Mouse On A Mirror
& OTHER CONTEMPORARY CHARACTER PIECES

BY PHILLIP KEVEREN

CONTENTS

2	Mouse On a Mirror
4	Quick Spin In A Fast Car
8	A Misty Morning
11	Summer Cloudburst
14	Downhill Daredevil

Editor: Margaret Otwell

ISBN 0-634-05570-4

7777 W. BLUEMOUND RD. P.O.BOX 13819 MILWAUKEE, WI 53213

In Australia Contact:
Hal Leonard Australia Pty. Ltd.
22 Taunton Drive P.O. Box 5130
Cheltenham East, 3192 Victoria, Australia
Email: ausadmin@halleonard.com

Copyright © 2003 by HAL LEONARD CORPORATION
International Copyright Secured All Rights Reserved

For all works contained herein:
Unauthorized copying, arranging, adapting, recording or public performance is an infringement of copyright.
Infringers are liable under the law.

Visit Hal Leonard Online at
www.halleonard.com

Mouse On A Mirror

By Phillip Keveren

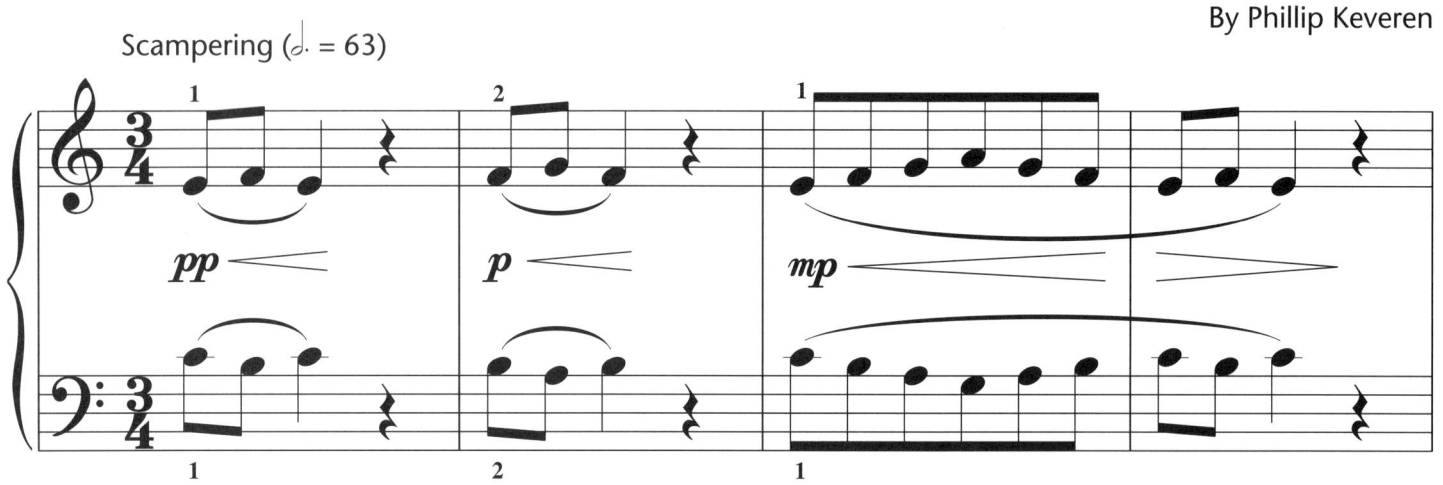

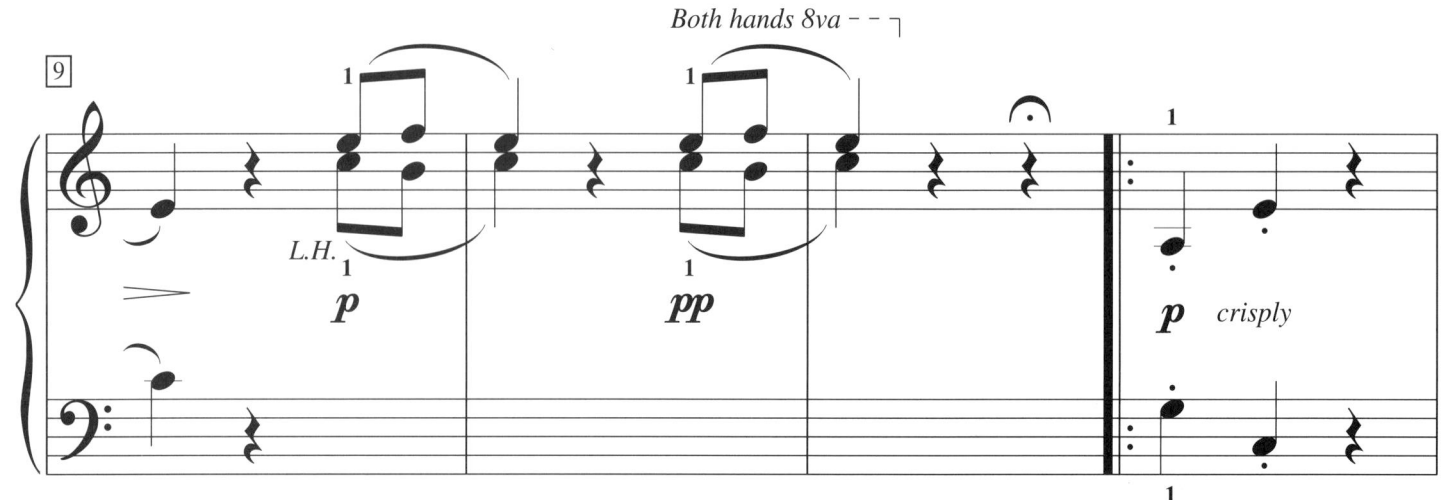

Quick Spin in a Fast Car

As fast as you dare! ($\dot{}$ = 69-72)

By Phillip Keveren

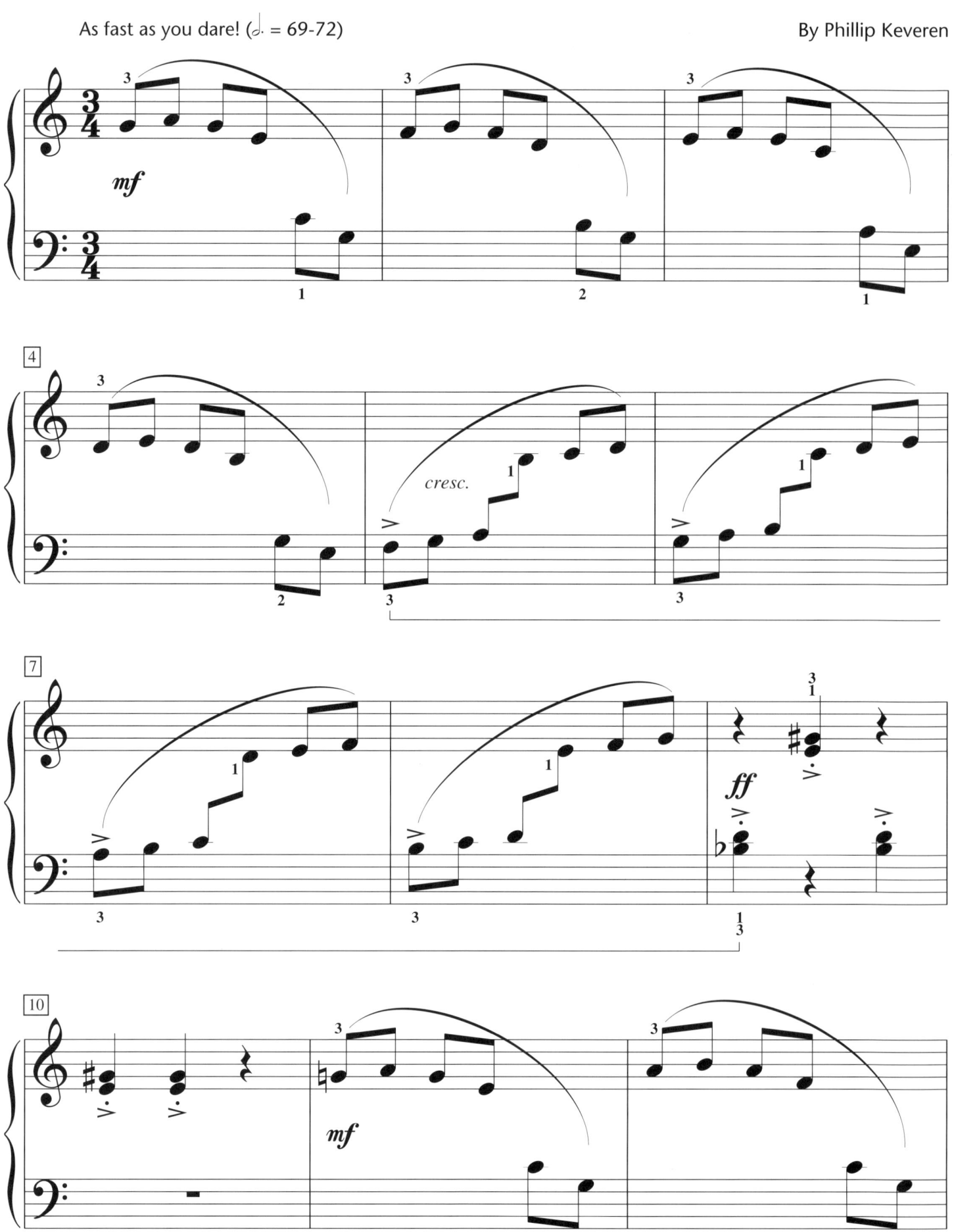

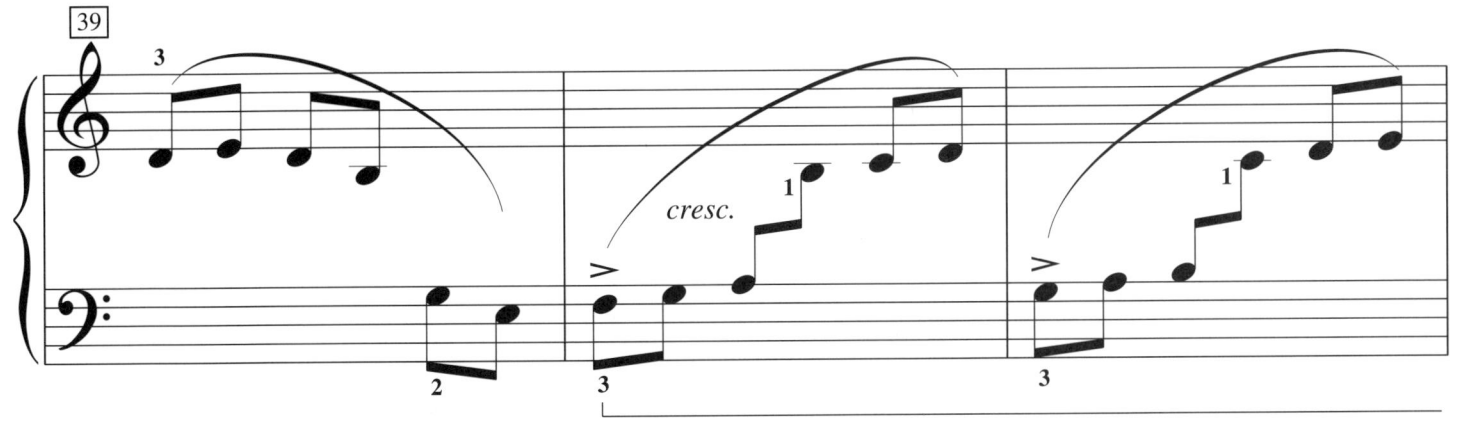
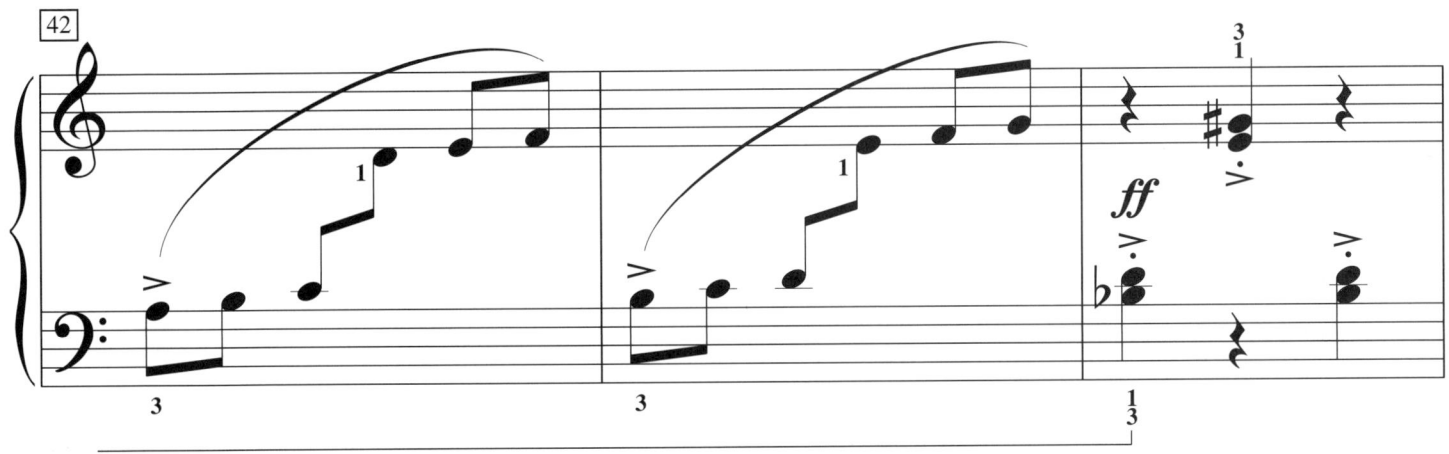
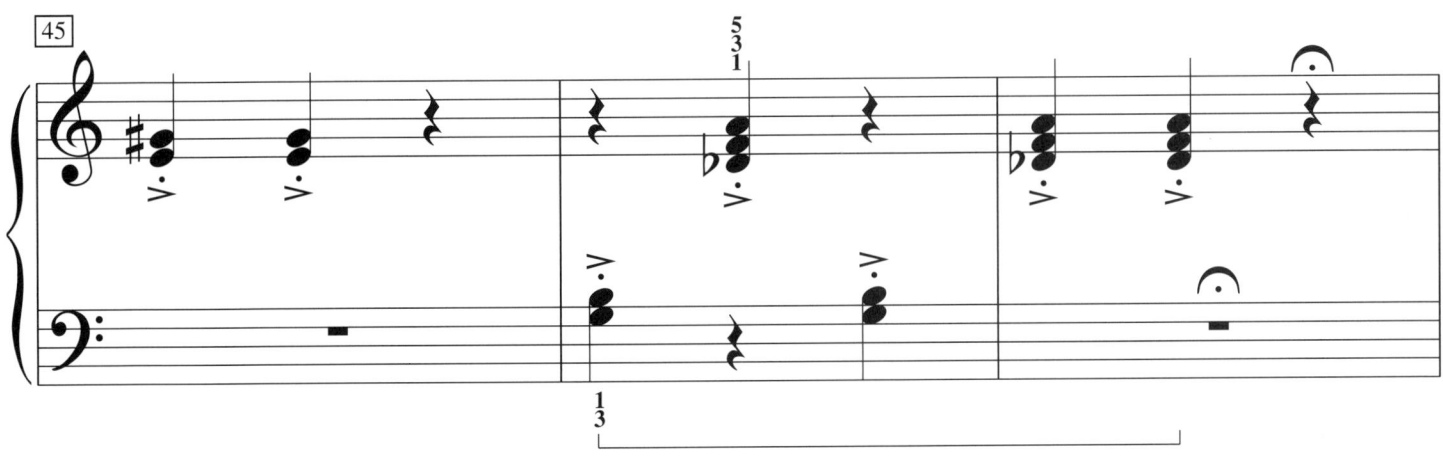

A Misty Morning

By Phillip Keveren

Slowly and spaciously, freely expressive (♩ c. 92)

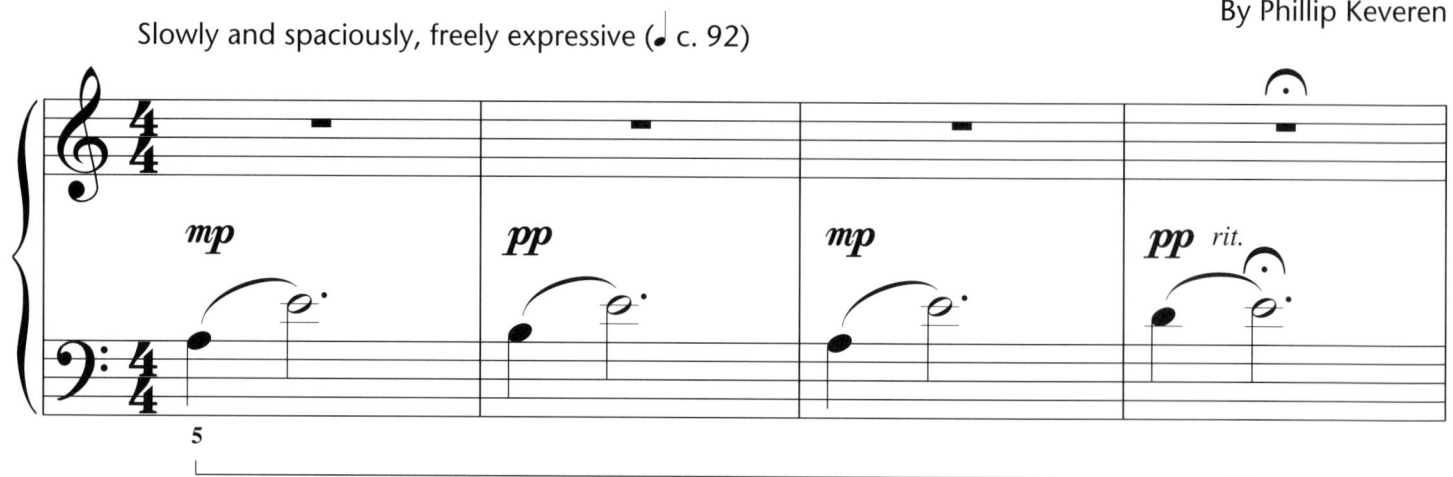
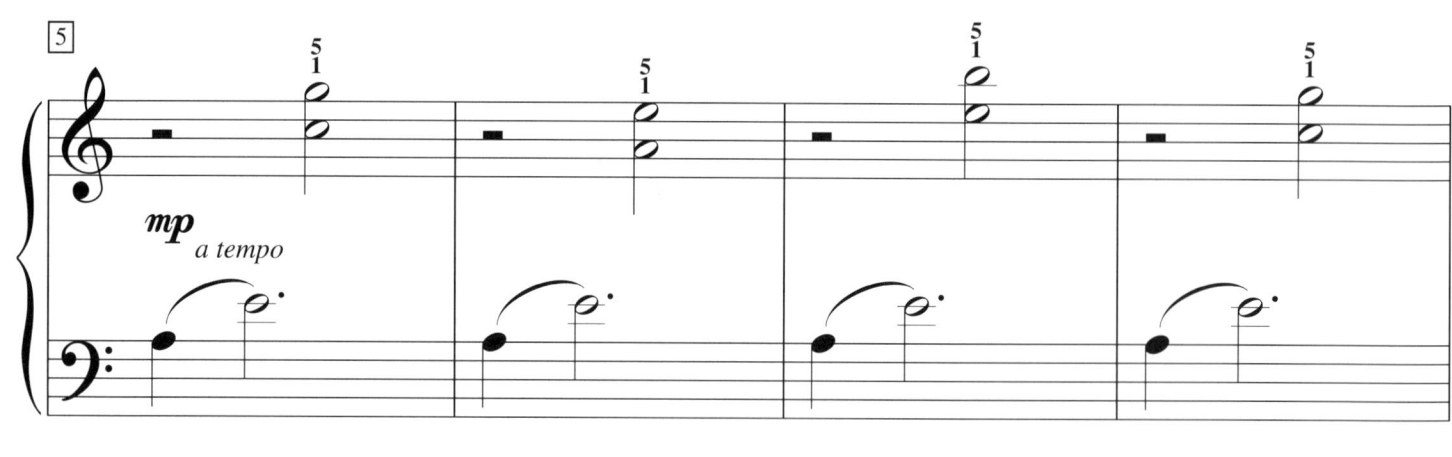
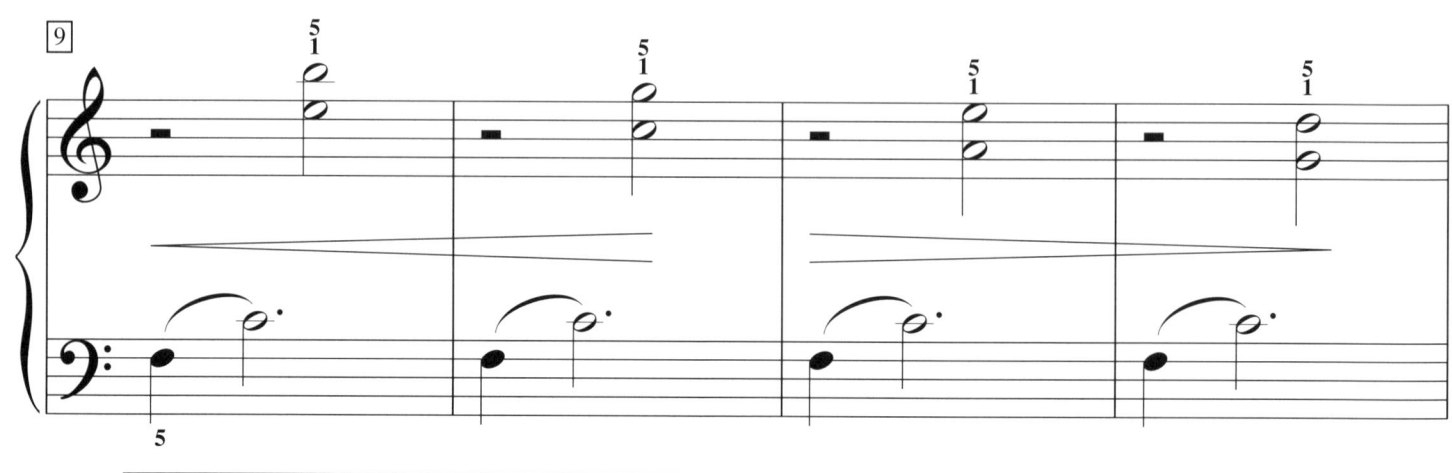

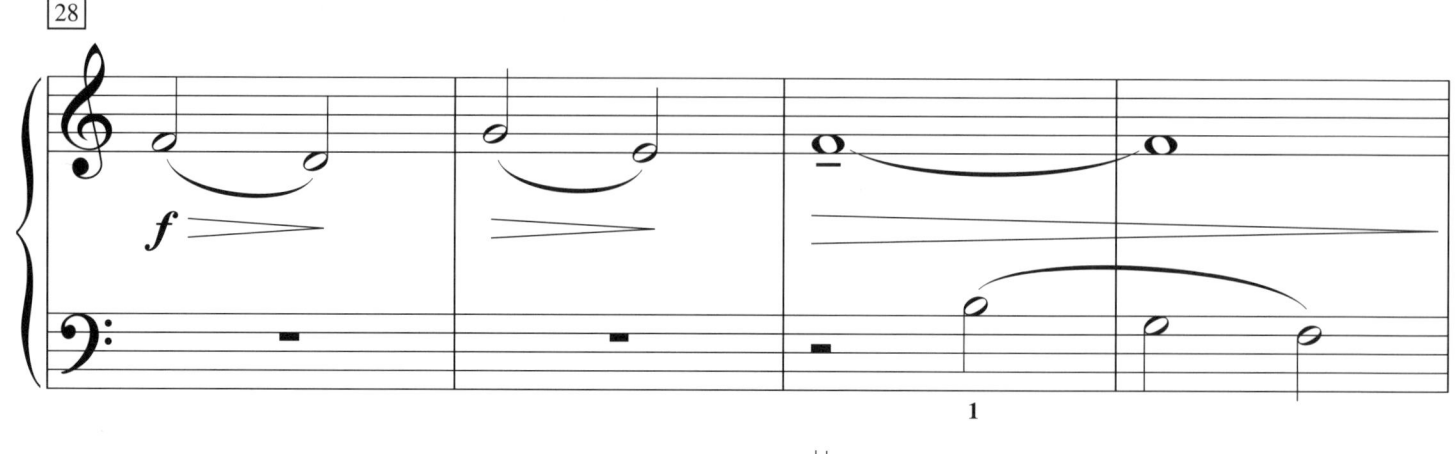
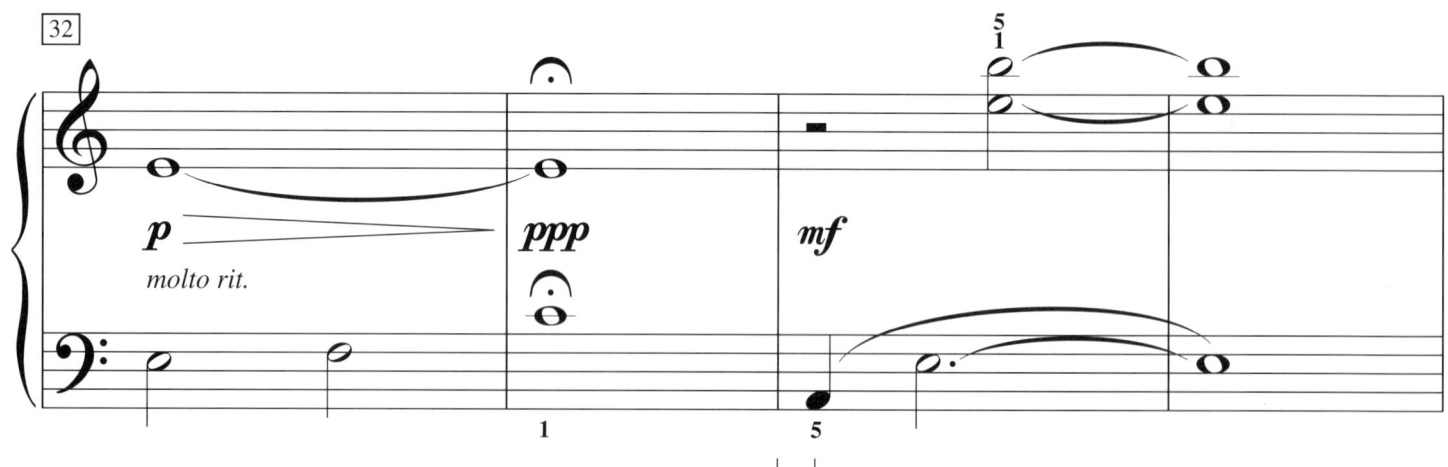
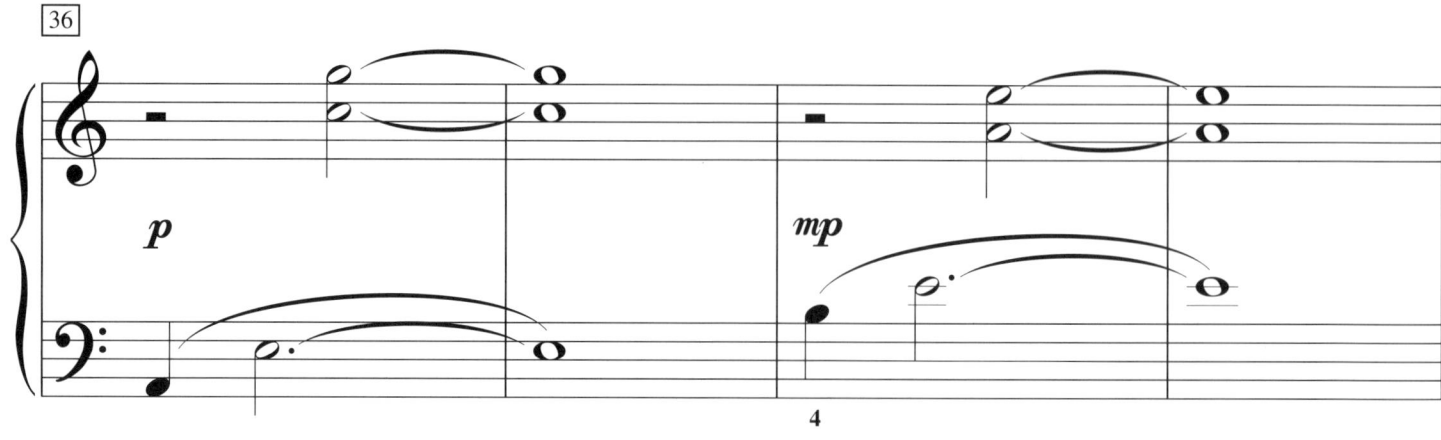
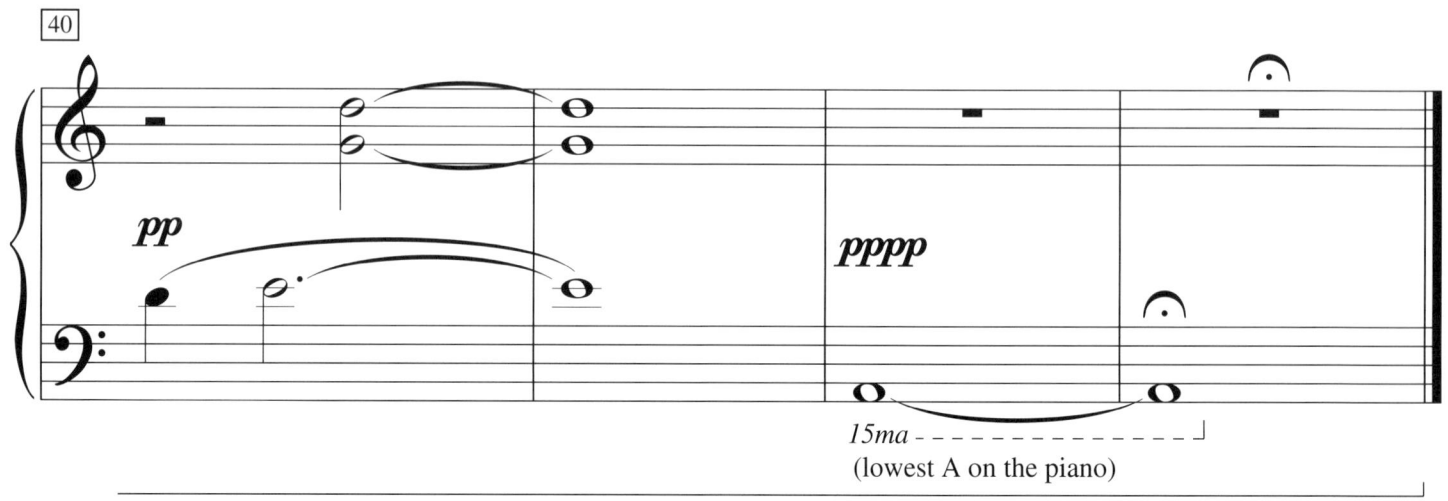

Summer Cloudburst

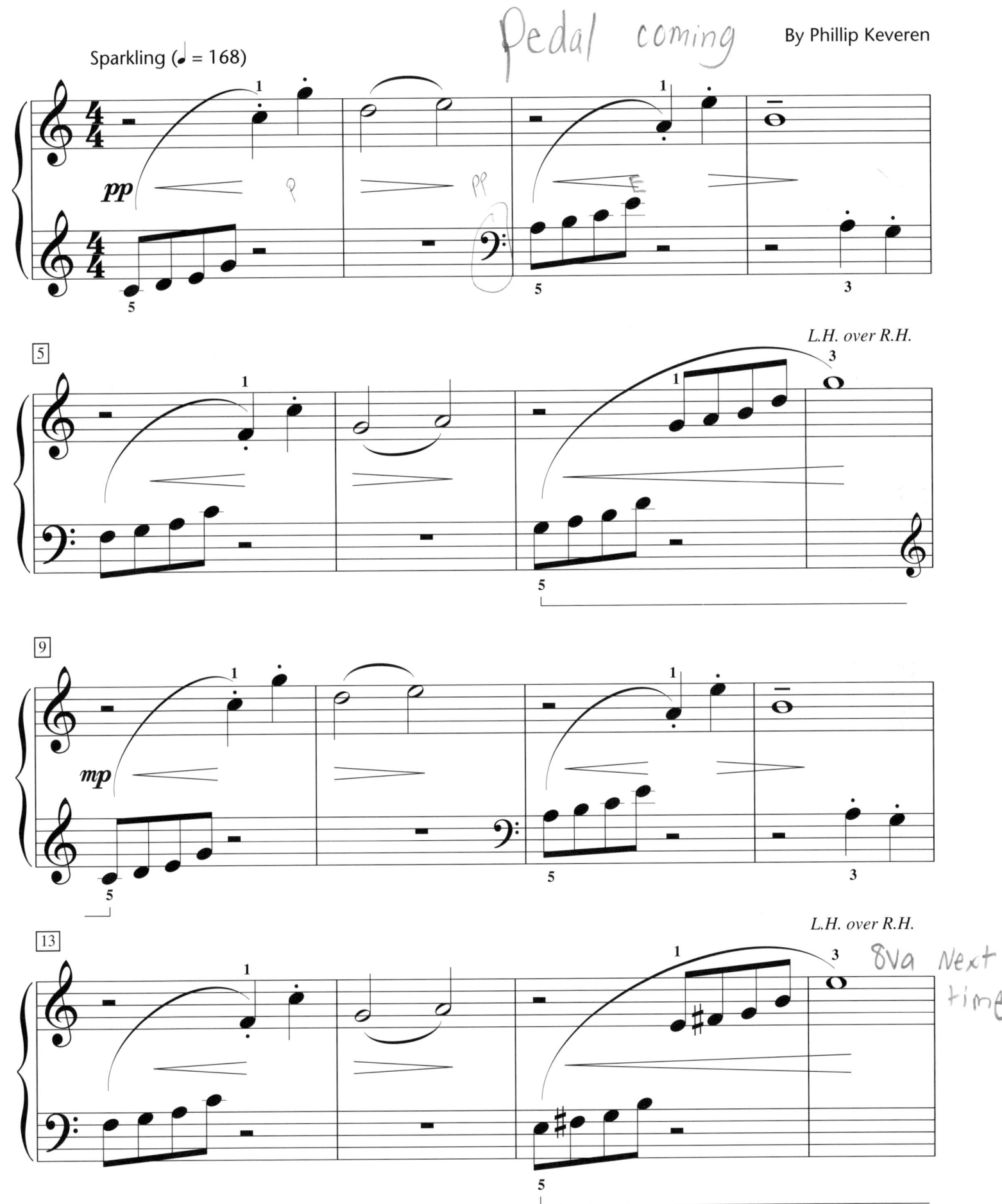#

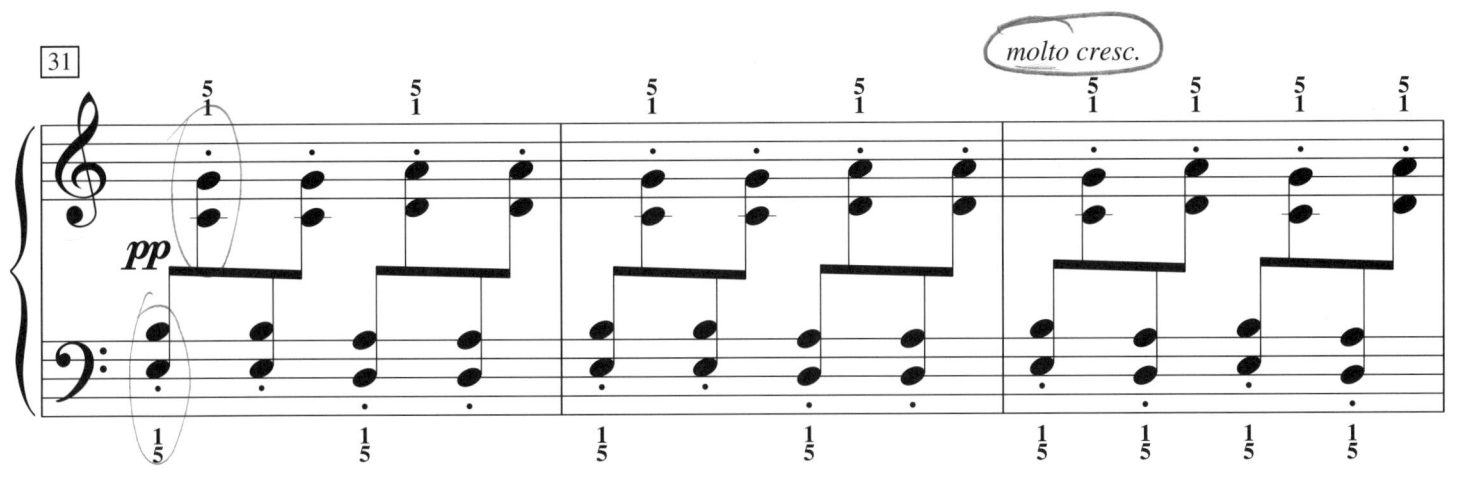
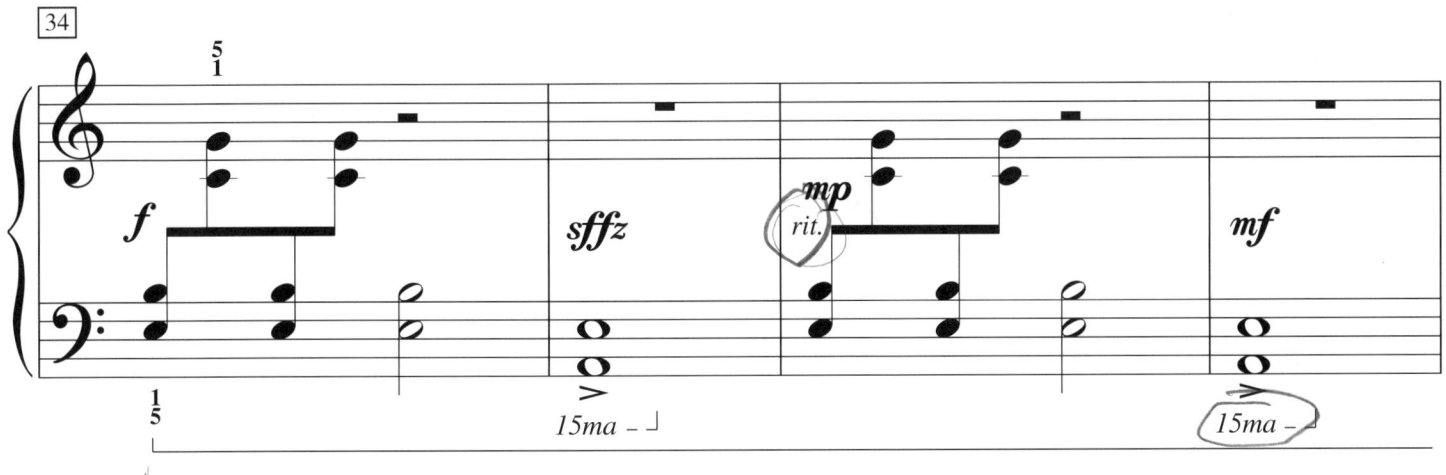
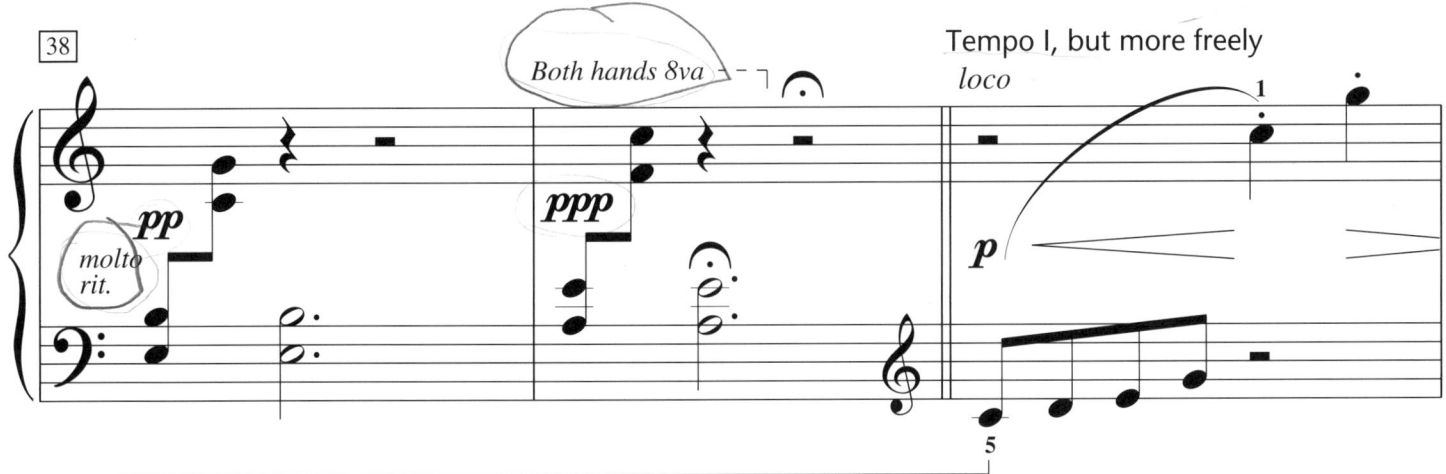
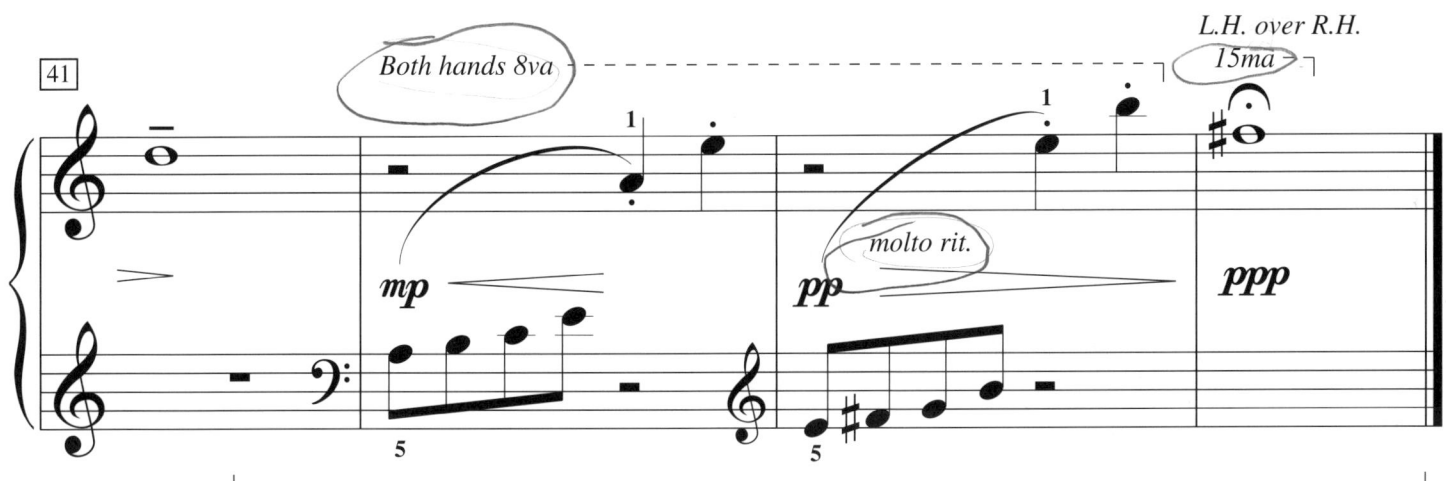

Downhill Daredevil

By Phillip Keveren

16
p
19
R.H.
f
R.H. over L.H.
L.H.
p
23
pp poco a poco cresc.
27
f
R.H. over L.H.
sffz
R.H. over L.H.
L.H.
8va

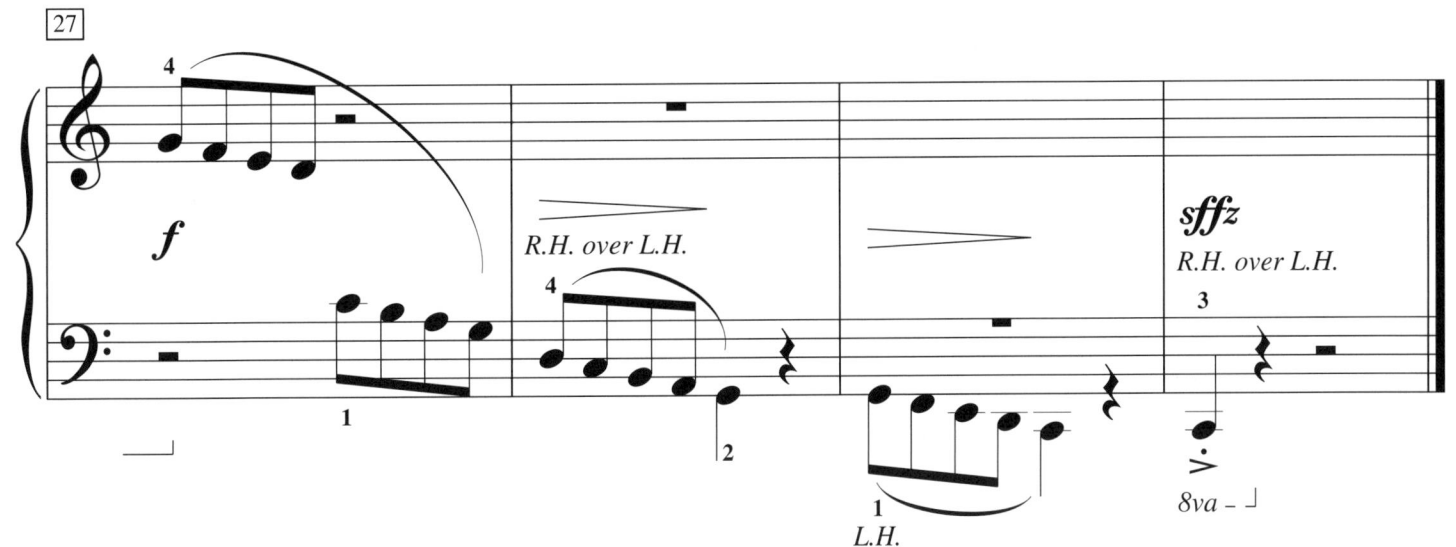

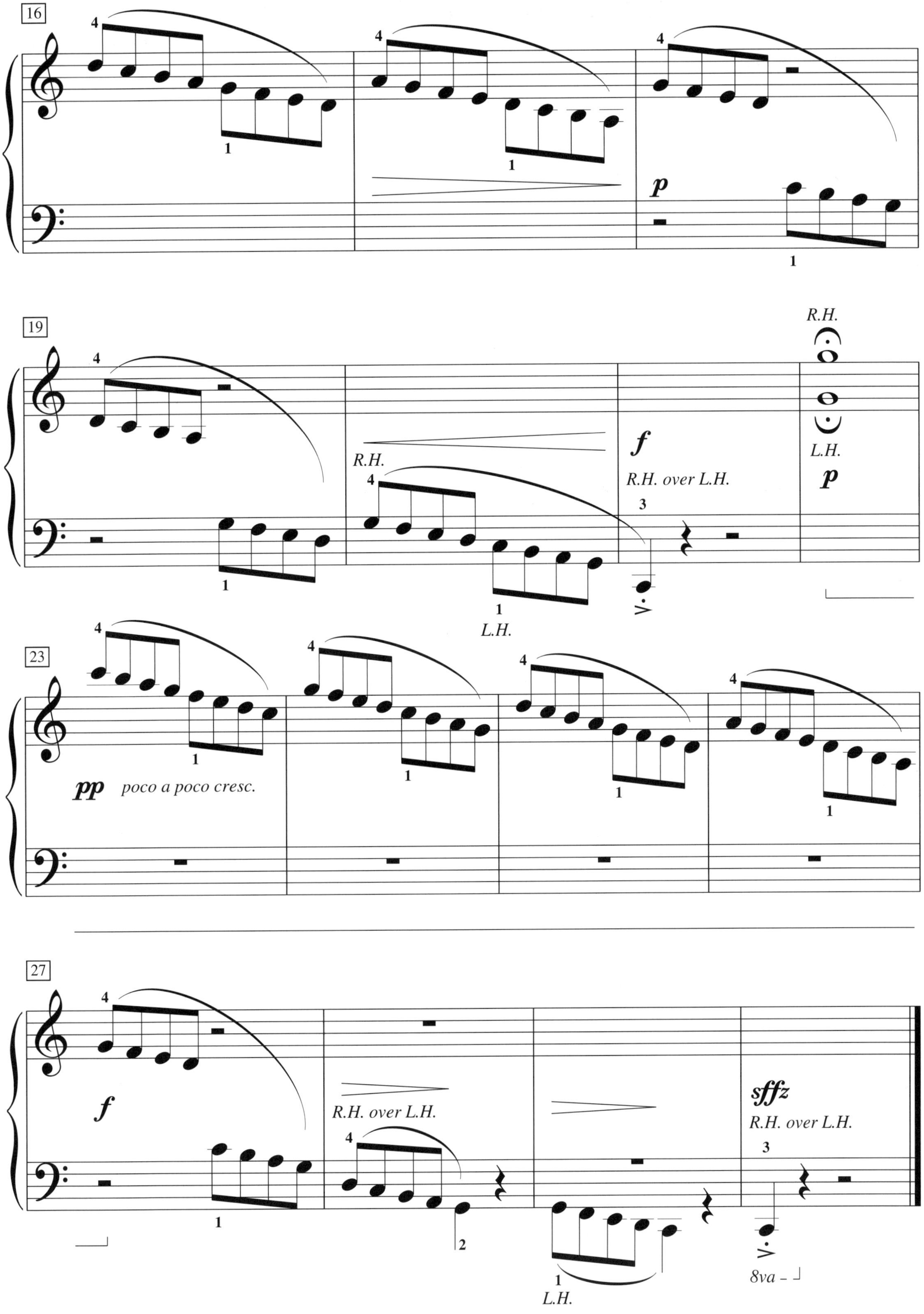

Composer Showcase Series

This series showcases the varied talents of our Hal Leonard Student Piano Library family of composers.

Here is where you will find great original piano music by your favorite composers, including Phillip Keveren, Carol Klose, Jennifer Linn, Bill Boyd, Bruce Berr, and many others. Carefully graded and leveled for easy selection, each book contains gems that are certain to become tomorrow's classics!

For a full description and songlist for each of the books listed here, and to view the newest titles in this series, visit our website at www.halleonard.com

For More Information,
See Your Local Music Dealer,
Or Write To:

HAL•LEONARD®
CORPORATION
7777 W. BLUEMOUND RD. P.O. BOX 13819
MILWAUKEE, WISCONSIN 53213

Prices, contents & availability subject to change without notice.

ELEMENTARY
Jazz Starters I
by Bill Boyd
HL00290425   10 Solos $6.95

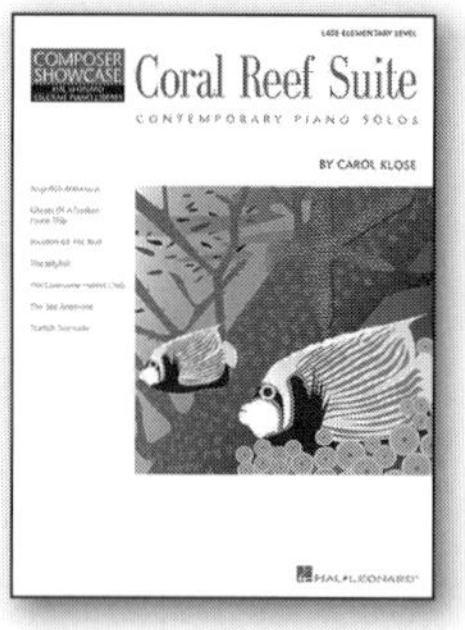

LATE ELEMENTARY
Coral Reef Suite
by Carol Klose
HL00296354   7 Solos $5.95

Imaginations In Style
by Bruce Berr
HL00290359   7 Solos $5.95

Jazz Starters II
by Bill Boyd
HL00290434   11 Solos $6.95

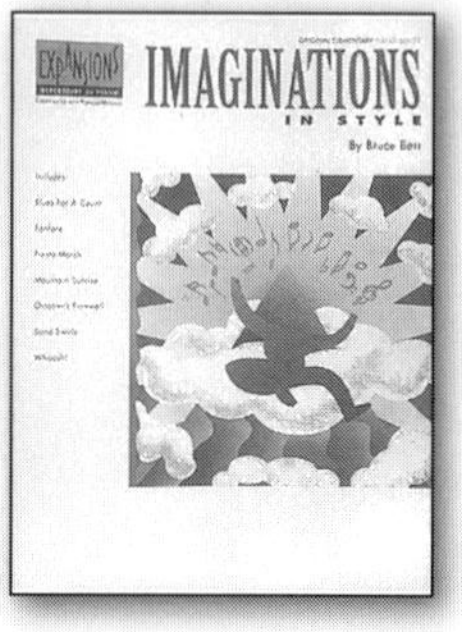

Jazz Starters III
by Bill Boyd
HL00290465   12 Solos $6.95

Mouse On A Mirror & Other Contemporary Character Pieces
by Phillip Keveren
HL00296361   ....$6.95

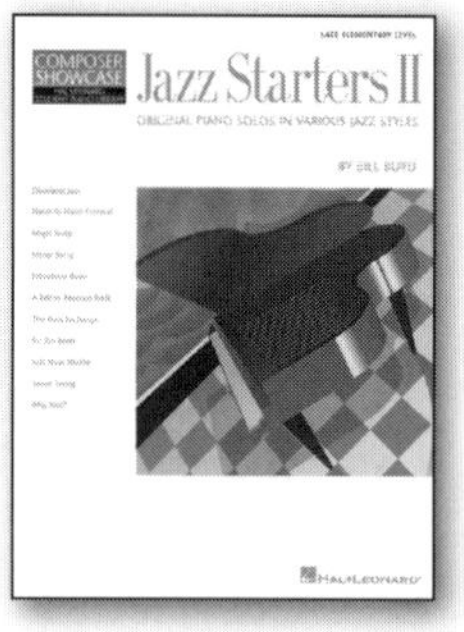

Tex-Mex Rex
by Phillip Keveren
HL00296353   6 Solos $5.95

EARLY INTERMEDIATE
Explorations In Style
by Bruce Berr
HL00290360   9 Solos $6.95

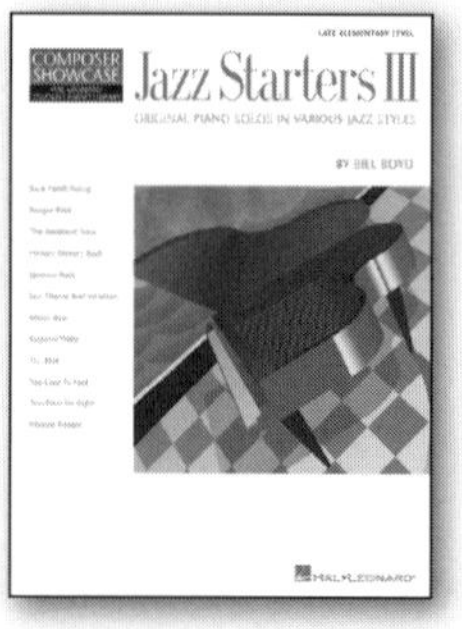

Monday's Child
by Deborah Brady
HL00296373..$6.95

INTERMEDIATE
Concerto For Young Pianists
by Matthew Edwards
HL00296356   2 Piano/4 Hands.....................$9.95

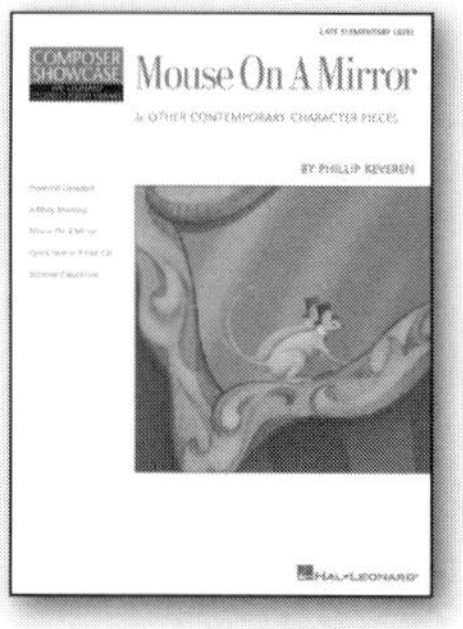

Jazz Delights
by Bill Boyd
HL00240435   11 Solos $6.95

Les Petites Impressions
by Jennifer Linn
HL00296355   6 Solos $6.95

0103

Unit 10 | Language Elements in Review

Language Arts 810
Language Elements in Review

INTRODUCTION |3

1. LANGUAGE   5

HISTORY |6
GRAMMAR |7
WORDS |13
USAGE |15
SENTENCES |16
PARAGRAPHS |18
LETTERS |20
COMPOSITIONS |22
SPELLING |26
SELF TEST 1 |29

2. COMMUNICATION   31

UNSPOKEN FACTORS IN COMMUNICATION |31
SPOKEN FACTORS OF COMMUNICATION |36
COMPREHENDING COMMUNICATION |39
SPELLING |41
SELF TEST 2 |44

3. READING   47

WORD PARTS |48
CONTEXT CLUES |49
SEQUENCE |50
FACT AND OPINION |51
NEWS ARTICLES |52
ESSAYS |55
AUTOBIOGRAPHIES |56
SPELLING |58
SELF TEST 3 |63

LIFEPAC Test is located in the center of the booklet. Please remove before starting the unit.

|1

Author:
Gail Lindenberg

Editor-in-Chief:
Richard W. Wheeler, M.A.Ed.

Editor:
Helen Robertson Prewitt, M.A.Ed.

Consulting Editor:
Larry Howard, Ed.D.

Revision Editor:
Alan Christopherson, M.S.

Westover Studios Design Team:
Phillip Pettet, Creative Lead
Teresa Davis, DTP Lead
Nick Castro
Andi Graham
Jerry Wingo
Lauren Faulk

804 N. 2nd Ave. E.
Rock Rapids, IA 51246-1759

© MCMXCVI by Alpha Omega Publications, Inc. All rights reserved.
LIFEPAC is a registered trademark of Alpha Omega Publications, Inc.

All trademarks and/or service marks referenced in this material are the property of their respective owners. Alpha Omega Publications, Inc. makes no claim of ownership to any trademarks and/or service marks other than their own and their affiliates, and makes no claim of affiliation to any companies whose trademarks may be listed in this material, other than their own.

Unit 10 | **Language Elements in Review**

Language Elements in Review

Introduction

The most important elements of language include the ability to speak, read, and write. Basic language skills and mastery of language usage make it possible for an individual to communicate effectively. Understanding each other is what allows humans to share ideas, to learn from each other, and to grow in knowledge. Communication is one of the most important parts of Christian life.

This LIFEPAC® is a review of the basic elements of the first nine LIFEPACs in the Language Arts 800 series. In this LIFEPAC you will look again at certain elements of language structure and usage. You will study language history, grammar, and writing forms. You will go over such factors of spoken and unspoken communication as gestures, listening, and speaking. You will study certain reading aids and various forms of nonfiction literature. You will also review words from the previous nine Language Arts LIFEPACs in the Spelling Word Review.

Objectives

Read these objectives. The objectives tell you what you will be able to do when you have successfully completed this LIFEPAC. When you have finished this LIFEPAC, you should be able to:

1. Trace the origin of the English language.
2. Correctly identify five parts of speech.
3. Explain some of the rules of grammar concerning correct punctuation, capitalization, and abbreviation.
4. Explain when to spell out numbers and figures.
5. Define the specific uses of the dictionary.
6. Describe the purpose of a thesaurus.
7. Explain the difference between standard and nonstandard English.
8. Identify and correct three types of sentence errors.
9. Explain the elements of a good paragraph.
10. List the two main categories of letters.
11. Explain the elements of a good essay.
12. List three unspoken factors of communication.
13. Name three basic purposes of speeches.
14. Correctly identify word parts as prefix, suffix, or root.
15. Explain ways to unlock word meanings.
16. Identify a statement as fact or opinion.
17. Explain sequence.
18. State the main purpose of a news article.
19. State the main purpose of an essay.
20. List three elements of autobiography.
21. Spell the review words correctly.

Language Elements in Review | Unit 10

Survey the LIFEPAC. Ask yourself some questions about this study and write your questions here.

1. LANGUAGE

Mastery of speaking, reading, and writing skills is very important to the person who wishes to express themself well and to communicate effectively with other people. In this section you will review the tools for using the written language properly. You will look at certain aspects of the history of the English language. You will use a dictionary and a thesaurus as word-finding tools. You will review the parts of speech as well as the rules of sentence structure, paragraph and essay writing, punctuation, capitalization, and forms of letter writing.

SECTION OBJECTIVES

Review these objectives. When you have completed this section, you should be able to:

1. Trace the origin of the English language.
2. Correctly identify five parts of speech.
3. Explain some of the rules of grammar concerning correct punctuation, capitalization, and abbreviation.
4. Explain when to spell out numbers and figures.
5. Define three specific uses of the dictionary.
6. Describe the purpose of a thesaurus.
7. Explain the difference between standard and nonstandard English.
8. Identify and correct three types of sentence errors.
9. Explain the elements of a good paragraph.
10. List the two main categories of letters.
11. Explain the elements of a good essay.
21. Spell the review words correctly.

VOCABULARY

Study these words to enhance your learning success in this section.

brainstorming (brān´ stôrm ing). Generation and collection of ideas.

coherent (kō hir´ unt). Having a logical connection or consistency.

dialects (dī´ u lekts). The local characteristics of speech that deviate from a standard language, usually developed in an isolated geographic region.

etymology (et u mol´ u jē). History of words.

homonym (hom´ u nim). A word having the same pronunciation or spelling as another word but a different meaning.

superimposed (sü pur im pozd´). One thing placed over another.

Note: *All vocabulary words in this LIFEPAC appear in* **boldface** *print the first time they are used. If you are not sure of the meaning when you are reading, study the definitions given.*

Pronunciation Key: hat, āge, cāre, fär; let, ēqual, tėrm; it, īce; hot, ōpen, ôrder; oil; out; cup, put, rüle; child; long; thin; /ŦH/ for then; /zh/ for measure; /u/ represents /a/ in about, /e/ in taken, /i/ in pencil, /o/ in lemon, and /u/ in circus.

Section 1 | 5

Language Elements in Review | Unit 10

HISTORY

Language began when God gave man the gift of speech so that people would be able to share their thoughts and knowledge. Words are merely symbols that refer to the things God created. Each item in God's world can be identified by a written and an oral symbol. Language is an important gift that separates man from the animals. The study of how that language developed into the language we use today is a fascinating one.

Origin. The roots of English language and literature are found in the period of history dating from about A.D. 449 to A.D. 1066. Old English was an inflected language. Old English did not depend on word order for meaning. Basically a Germanic language, English has a strong Latin influence. Many current usages can be traced to a Latin root word. Tracing the history of a particular word is known as **etymology**.

The English language that we speak today developed from Indo-European languages. Scientists who study languages have determined many distinct relationships among the European languages and have traced the original words to the parent language, Indo-European. The languages altered with geographical location as different people used the words in different ways. Several **dialects** emerged in this fashion.

Nature. The nature of current English language is a result of many influences. As a country was invaded, the conquerors brought their own languages with them. Often the language of the conquering armies was **superimposed** over the language of the invaded area. In 1066 the Norman Invasion brought French influence into England. Gradually the London dialect took precedence over other dialects because of London's vast population and influence. Our Modern English has evolved directly from this London dialect. For more information see Language Arts LIFEPACs 802, 806, and 809.

 Complete these activities.

1.1 Read Genesis chapter 2, and find references to the first words spoken by man.

　a. What was the reason for Adam's use of language in Genesis 2:19–20?
　_____

　b. Explain the situation in Genesis 2:23.
　_____
　_____

1.2 Name the parent language of current English. _____

Answer true or false.

1.3 _____ Modern English evolved from the London dialect.

1.4 _____ English is a Latin language.

1.5 _____ Indo-European was the parent language.

1.6 _____ Old English was inflected.

1.7 _____ The Normans introduced Germanic influence in 1066.

6 | Section 1

Unit 10 | **Language Elements in Review**

GRAMMAR

Grammar is the study of the specific rules of language. Anyone who is willing to exert a little honest effort and concentration can strengthen their ability to apply grammar rules to the language they use every day.

Classifications. Eight basic classifications for English words include noun, pronoun, verb, adverb, adjective, interjection, conjunction, and preposition. Each word group serves a specific purpose in the structure of language. If you have difficulties with any parts of speech, refer to Language Arts LIFEPAC 802. Five parts of speech you have studied are included in the following review.

Nouns are words that name things. A common noun is the name of a person, place, or thing. A proper noun names a specific person, place, or thing. Proper nouns are always capitalized. Every real object in God's world can be named. Ideas can also be given names. Concrete nouns are things you can touch; abstract nouns stand for ideas or qualities you cannot touch.

- **Concrete nouns:** hamburger, chair, puppy
- **Abstract nouns:** love, holiness, happiness

Verbs show action or state of being in a sentence. Auxiliary verbs help a main verb express certain meanings, forms, or tenses.

- **Verbs:** ran, jump, pranced, had gone, have seen

Pronouns take the place of nouns. Without pronouns our language would be cluttered with the repetition of the names of things.

Examples:

- John looked for *John's* book in *John's* locker.
- John looked for *his* book in *his* locker.

Remember that pronouns may be *personal* and may be used as subjects, objects, or possessive forms. *Personal compound pronouns,* formed by adding *-self* or *-selves* to the personal pronoun forms, may be reflexive or intensive. Other types of pronouns include *interrogative* (who, what, which, whose), *demonstrative* (this, that, these), *indefinite* (anyone, each, others), and *relative* (who, which, that).

- **Reflexive pronoun:** I hurt *myself.* (refers to the subject)
- **Intensive pronoun:** She made the dress *herself.* (emphasizes the subject)
- **Interrogative pronoun:** *What* did you say?
- **Demonstrative pronoun:** *Those* are nice, but I like *these* better.
- **Indefinite pronoun:** *Anyone* in the class may borrow these books.
- **Relative pronoun:** The book *that* is open is mine.

	Subject Pronouns	**Object Pronouns**	**Possessive Pronouns**
	I	me	my, mine
singular	you	you	your, yours
	he, she, it	him, her, it	his, hers, its
	we	us	our, ours
plural	you	you	your, yours
	they	them	their, theirs

Section 1 | **7**

Language Elements in Review | Unit 10

Adjectives are words that describe or modify nouns. Adjectives answer the questions *What kind? How many? Which one?* The articles *a, an,* and *the* are adjectives.

Examples:

- Alicia found the *red* book. (Which one?)
- We have *ten* dogs. (How many?)
- Throw this *filthy* thing away! (What kind?)

Adverbs modify or change verbs, adjectives, or other adverbs. Adverbs answer the questions *When? Where? How?* and *How much?* or *How often?*

Examples:

- The girl *gladly* read the announcement. (How?)
- John *repeatedly* missed the question. (How much?/How often?)

 Complete these activities.

1.8 Circle the nouns in the following passage. (13 nouns)

Now when Jesus was born in Bethlehem of Judea in the days of Herod the king, behold, there came wise men from the east to Jerusalem. Saying, Where is he that is born King of the Jews? For we have seen his star in the east, and are come to worship him. (Matthew 2:1 and 2).

1.9 Underline the verbs and verb forms in the following passage. (11 verbs)

And the whole multitude of them arose, and led him unto Pilate. And they began to accuse him, saying, We found this fellow perverting the nation, and forbidding to give tribute to Caesar, saying that he himself is Christ, a King. (Luke 23: 1 and 2)

1.10 Write *X* on each repeated noun (and its article) and replace it with an appropriate pronoun.

a. The Bible tells us that the Bible is the Word of God.

b. The flower had hardly opened before the flower's petals began to drop.

c. Alice asked Mary, "Will Mary have lunch with Alice?"

d. The members of the congregation prepared the members of the congregation for silent prayer.

1.11 Underline the adjectives except *a, an,* and *the* in the following paragraph. (16 adjectives)

This story is an unusual one. It tells of a miraculous event which occurred many years ago. A little town called Bethlehem was the setting for this blessed event. A tired and weary couple found warm refuge in a stable. In the warmth of the clean straw among the friendly beasts, a child was born to the young woman. A bright, new star rose above the town and signaled to all the world that this birth was very special. Indeed, the Christ was born.

8 | Section 1

For each sentence write (a) the word modified and (b) the adverb.

1.12 In Bethlehem the angels gladly reported the birth of Jesus.

a. _____   b. _____

1.13 King Herod looked anxiously for the Christ child.

a. _____   b. _____

1.14 The wise men headed excitedly toward the new star.

a. _____   b. _____

Punctuation. Punctuation symbols are the regulatory signs of the English language. The symbols tell you certain things about what you are reading. Punctuation ends thoughts, links ideas, interrupts thoughts, indicates a question, or emphasizes a certain idea within a written text. Punctuation marks help the reader understand what the author intends.

Three common punctuation marks are the period, the question mark, and the exclamation point. These marks end a thought and indicate whether the sentence is a question, an exclamation, or a simple statement. Other useful punctuation marks are the comma, the semicolon, and the colon. Commas within a sentence are used to link a series of ideas, to show an interruption of the thought, or to aid a conjunction in linking two independent thoughts. The semicolon can link two closely related independent clauses without a conjunction or with a conjunctive adverb. The semicolon is stronger than a comma, but weaker than a period. The colon is a mark which signals that information is about to follow. The colon often follows an independent clause that ends in a noun. Colons are useful in preparing the reader for important facts. The following examples show the proper use of each of these punctuation marks.

Examples:

- I see her coming.
- Have you ever been to Kansas?
- We won!
- I ate a hot dog, potato chips, and slaw.
- He is, indeed, late for the program.
- He wanted to have a picnic, but it rained all day.
- Arizona has many natural wonders; therefore, the state is quite popular with tourists.
- When we went to Washington, D.C., we saw these places of interest: the White House, the Library of Congress, the Smithsonian Institute, and the Washington Monument.

If you have difficulty with any of the punctuation marks and the usage of punctuation, refer to Language Arts LIFEPACs 803 and 805.

Capitalization. Another important technical element of good writing is capitalization. The rules for capitalization are quite simple. If you have difficulties with capitalization, refer to Language Arts LIFEPAC 805.

The basic rules for using capital letters can be briefly summarized. A capital letter is used at the beginning of every sentence and for the first letter of all proper nouns. A capital letter is used for all important words in the titles of books. Capital letters are also used in reference to God and Christ.

LANGUAGE ELEMENTS IN REVIEW | Unit 10

1.15 Capitalize and punctuate the following letter and envelope.

june 24 20_ _

a. dear jill,

i can hardly wait to see you at camp ill be at camp inspiration on the sixteenth of this month i hope you are as excited about this retreat as i am dont forget to bring your tennis racquet swim suit and a bible last year camp was a real experience for me the way we shared our love of christ was as inspiring as the beautiful surroundings of the pine forest ill bet thats why its called camp inspiration look for me on july 16

yours in christ

sally simpson

b. sally simpson
247 norfolk way
allen town mo 63001

jill baker
426 w elm st
phoenix az 85007

10 | Section 1

Abbreviations. When a word is shortened, it becomes an abbreviation. Every abbreviation needs a period at the end of each part. Abbreviations should be avoided in formal writing. Knowing common abbreviated symbols is important in mastery of current English usage. Agencies and organizations are often referred to by the abbreviation of their titles known as *acronyms*. Acronyms are used as words; therefore, acronyms are not punctuated. The abbreviation for the names of U.S. states is two capital letters without any periods.

Examples:

- The P.T.A. will meet at 7:00 tonight. (P.T.A. is an abbreviation.)
- NASA announced the successful launch. (NASA is an acronym.)

Numbers and figures. Numbers and figures sometimes cause problems for writers. A good rule of thumb is to spell out numbers under 100 and use the numeral symbols for any number in excess of 100. Exceptions to this general rule appear in the use of dates, addresses, room numbers, hours of the day, and mathematics or science problems.

- **Example**: Three people went to 280 S. Fifth Ave. at 6:30 a.m.

Answer these questions.

1.16 What are acronyms? _____

1.17 Which numbers should by spelled out in writing a paragraph? _____

1.18 What form of punctuation usually ends an abbreviation? _____

Complete these activities. Use a dictionary if necessary.

1.19 Correct these abbreviations and numbers.

   a. The Brown Co _____

   b. Box fourteen _____

   c. Greenton, Il _____

1.20 Write the abbreviation for these words.

   a. captain _____   b. post office _____

   c. pound _____   d. et cetera _____

Section 1 | **11**

Language Elements in Review | Unit 10

In Language Arts LIFEPAC 805, you studied three other types of punctuation: the apostrophe, the hyphen, quotation marks, parentheses, and italics.

The apostrophe is used to show possession or to indicate contractions. The possessive is formed by adding *'s* to a singular noun or to a plural noun not ending in *s*. Add an apostrophe to plural nouns ending in *s*. Study the following examples of forming possessives.

Examples:
- man + 's = man's
- children + 's = children's
- ladies + ' = ladies'

In contractions, the apostrophe shows the omission of one or more letters. Notice the way the following contractions are formed.

Examples:
- cannot = can't
- would not = wouldn't

In some parts of the United States certain *dialectal* differences in pronunciation result in unpronounced letters. Frequently a final consonant is not pronounced, as in *saying* (sayin') and *going* (goin').

 Punctuate these sentences correctly.

1.21 Wont you hurry up, or arent you comin?

1.22 Im listenin but I cant hear you.

A hyphen is used to join the parts of a compound word (mother-in-law), compound numbers from twenty-one to ninety-nine (thirty-three), and fractions (one-half). Hyphens join figures in inclusive dates (1850-1921), divide a word into syllables at the end of a line (temper-ature), and come between certain prefixes, suffixes, and roots. A hyphen is used between a prefix and a proper noun (pro-Christian), between a prefix and root beginning and ending with the same vowel (re-echo), and between the suffix—*elect* and the root word (President-elect).

 Hyphenate this paragraph correctly.

1.23 My brother in law served in the army (1975 1978) as a special assistant to the commander in chief's staff advisors. His immediate superior had been in the service for twenty seven years. He had served under ex President Eisenhower during World War II. My brother in law is now a reporter and plans one day to be editor in chief of his paper. Since he is a stick to it type of person, he will probably succeed.

12 | Section 1

Unit 10 | **Language Elements in Review**

WORDS

The ability to choose a variety of words makes a writer better able to express themself. Learning to look for new words and using a variety of terms help to create a clear impression of what the writer is attempting to express.

Dictionary. The dictionary was first introduced in the United States by Noah Webster in 1806. A dictionary contains an alphabetical listing of words, keys to pronunciation, and definitions for these words. Some dictionaries also include the etymology, or history, of a word. A dictionary is a handy tool for the writer. A dictionary should be used to check spellings of words, to clarify meanings of words, and to make sure the written words are used properly.

Thesaurus. *Roget's International Thesaurus* is the most common book of this type used in America. A thesaurus is not a prehistoric animal; it is a book of synonyms and antonyms. A synonym is a word that has the same meaning; an antonym is a word with opposite meaning. *Small* and *little* are synonyms; *light* and *dark* are antonyms. The thesaurus is an alphabetical list of words. Each entry lists synonyms and antonyms for that word. A good writer will use a thesaurus to avoid repetition of words, to expand the vocabulary they use, and to locate words that express their exact meaning. Not included in the thesaurus is a third category of words, **homonyms**. Homonyms are words that sound alike but are spelled differently and have different meanings—such as *rain* and *reign*.

 Answer these questions.

1.24 How is the dictionary organized? _____

1.25 What are three things a dictionary tells you?

a. _____ b. _____ c. _____

1.26 Who wrote the first important United States dictionary? _____

1.27 What is the main purpose of a thesaurus? _____

_____

Write a paragraph.

1.28 Use your dictionary and thesaurus to paraphrase the Pledge of Allegiance and the Lord's Prayer (Matthew 6:9).

a. _____

_____

_____

_____

_____

_____

Section 1 | **13**

b. _____
_____
_____
_____
_____
_____
_____
_____
_____

Complete this activity.

1.29 Play a game with words.

a. You will need one or more other people and a dictionary. Each side should make up a list of twenty words or facts found in a dictionary. Trade lists with the other side. See which side can find the information more quickly.

b. Again you will need to have two or more people. Using your thesaurus or dictionary, play scrabble. If you do not have a set available, cut heavy paper or cardboard into 1-inch squares. Make four cards for each consonant and eight cards for each vowel. Now see how many words you can form from these cards following these rules:

- Two to 4 players in each group.
- Each player is given 10 squares (face down).
- The first player draws a square, forms a word from the squares in their hand, and discards one square.
- The play then goes to the person on their right who does the same, only they must make their word join the first word as in a crossword puzzle.
- Every word of less than five letters is worth 25 points.
- Every word of 5 to 10 letters is worth 35 points.
- Every word after 10 letters is worth 50 points.
- Any word that is unfamiliar to the group (you have never seen or heard of it, yet it is in the thesaurus or dictionary) is worth 50 points.
- Any word used that is *not* in the thesaurus or dictionary is worth -30 (you must subtract 30 points).

TEACHER CHECK _____ _____
                  initials   date

USAGE

English usage is usually divided into two levels, standard and nonstandard. Standard English is used by teachers, ministers , and any people in a formal setting. Standard English usage depends upon awareness of some of the common errors in language and upon avoiding such errors. If you have difficulties with errors in usage, refer to Language Arts LIFEPAC 804 and LIFEPAC 809.

Slang. The use of slang in formal situations is inappropriate because it changes the tone of your words, can create confusion, and weakens your message. Slang words are words that usually relate to something the users of slang have in common. Slang also includes shortened words, trendy words, and coinages. For example, friends that are talking about *insta* are using a shortened, trendy word, and they share a common interest in social media. Slang changes quickly depending on what is popular and happening in the world. Slang should be avoided unless you know that it is acceptable in the given situation.

Double negatives. A double negative is the incorrect use of two negatives in the same sentence.

- **Example**: I have*n't no* quarter.

The problem in using double negatives is easily solved by eliminating one of the negative modifiers. If you want to correct a double negative, just remove one of the negatives.

- **Correct**: I have no quarter.
- **Correct**: I haven't a quarter.

Dangling modifiers. Mistakes in usage can be embarrassing. Misplaced modifiers often create sentence confusion.

- **Example**: Hanging from the ceiling by a single thread, Jane spotted a spider.

This type of error can be avoided by placing the modifier closest to the word it modifies.

- **Correct**: Jane spotted a spider hanging from the ceiling by a single thread.

Shifts. A final area of common errors in usage include shifts in person, mood, and tense. The mood of a verb refers to the way that action or emotion is stated. A shift in tense confuses the time and makes the reader wonder what is happening when. A shift in person is a change of voice. This shift confuses the reader and makes them wonder who is speaking or writing.

- **Shift in mood**: Stop talking and can you listen more closely?
- **Right**: Stop talking and listen more closely. (Both are imperative.)
- **Right**: Can you stop talking and listen more closely? (Both are indicative.)

| Misplaced Modifiers

- **Shift in tense**: Alice ran out the door and falls over a skate.
- **Right**: Alice ran out the door and fell over a skate.
- **Right**: Alice runs out the door and falls over a skate.

- **Shift in person**: If you come from a good home, one should be thankful.
- **Right**: If you come from a good home, you should be thankful.
- **Right**: If one comes from a good home, they should be thankful.

In this last example, the *singular they* is used because the gender is not specified. The singular use of *they* and *their* is officially accepted in grammar style guides. The key to avoiding any kind of shift in usage is to be consistent.

 Write the following sentences correctly using Standard English.

1.30 I haven't got no quarter.
_____

1.31 We can't hardly see the sky.
_____

1.32 A natural disaster, John thought the flood would make a good news story.
_____
_____

1.33 When a boy reaches high school, you must consider the future.
_____
_____

1.34 John and his friend did his homework.
_____

SENTENCES

A sentence is a group of words that makes a meaningful statement. The two basic sentence parts are the *subject*, or the naming part, and the *predicate*, or the telling part. The key word in the subject is usually a noun or pronoun. The key word in the predicate is usually a verb. Good sentence writing is the key to effective written communication. Three types of sentence errors commonly made include the comma splice, the run-on, and the fragment.

Comma splice. A common error in sentence writing is the comma splice problem, which is a result of incorrectly joining two or more sentences (independent clauses) with a comma. Comma splices usually occur when the ideas expressed are closely related.

- **Example**: Janet went to the library, Jean stayed home.

Unit 10 | **Language Elements in Review**

One way to avoid the comma splice is to separate the words into two distinct sentences. Another method of correction is to use a comma and a conjunction, creating a compound sentence.

- **Correct**: Janet went to the library. Jean stayed home.
- **Correct**: Janet went to the library, and Jean stayed home.

Run-on. A run-on sentence consists of several main clauses joined together by the excessive use of such conjunctions as *and* and *so*.

- **Example**: Janet went to the library *and* she checked out several books *and* Jean stayed home *so* she could study.

To correct a run-on sentence you may divide the ideas into separate sentences, use subordination, use coordination and subordination, or use a combination of methods.

Fragments. Another common sentence error in writing is the sentence fragment. A fragment is a piece of a sentence, usually a dependent clause or a sentence part. Something missing in the sentence fragment must be added to form a complete statement. To identify sentence fragments, you should ask yourself what is named in each sentence (subject). Then you should ask what is happening (predicate). If the sentence is complete, something is named and some action is taking place. Remember that a sentence must be an independent clause. A clause may have a subject and a predicate yet be a fragment.

- **Fragment**: on the way home
- **Fragment**: while he was on the way home
- **Sentence**: His car had a blowout while he was on the way home.

Complete these activities.

1.35 List the three most common types of sentence errors.

a. _____   b. _____   c. _____

1.36 List the two basic sentence elements.

a. _____   b. _____

1.37 Read the following sentences. On the line write *S* if it is a good sentence, *C-S* if it is a comma-splice sentence, *RO* if it is a run-on, and *F* if it is a sentence fragment.

a. _____ Saints, every one of them.

b. _____ You wash, I'll dry.

c. _____ We've tried several times to locate him and we called his friends and drove by his house so we could tell him you are here.

d. _____ Because she couldn't get her parents' permission.

e. _____ Not one person whom I met last night.

f. _____ Miss Smith kept both of them after school, they hadn't done their homework.

Section 1 | **17**

g. _____ Miss Smith kept both of them after school because they hadn't done their homework.

h. _____ It's not a cobra, it's a rattler.

i. _____ It's a cobra, not a rattler.

j. _____ Jesus wept.

k. _____ Sally ate and Lisa watched her so that Sally would clean her plate so that she could have dessert.

PARAGRAPHS

A paragraph is a group of sentences written for a basic purpose. The purpose of each paragraph is the main idea expressed in the paragraph. Usually one sentence in the paragraph states the topic or main idea. The other sentences support the topic statement and add detail to the general idea expressed.

A paragraph may contain one sentence, or it may contain ten or more. Unless the author needs to emphasize an important idea by isolating it in a one-sentence paragraph, a paragraph of one sentence is to be avoided. By definition a paragraph is a *group* of related sentences.

A well-developed paragraph usually needs about five complete sentences. This number includes one topic sentence, three or more support (or detail) sentences, and a clincher statement which concludes the paragraph or provides a transition to the next paragraph.

If you wish to write a "perfect paragraph" every time, check for the following elements in your writing:

1. Always use a topic sentence.
2. Be sure all sentences relate to the topic.
3. Be sure that each paragraph is written for a specific purpose.
4. Make sure your paragraph is **coherent**.

Coherence is also an important element of paragraph writing. A coherent paragraph is organized logically. Using logical order for putting the details into a paragraph will help the reader to follow the train of your thoughts as you write.

Most good paragraphs are written in either chronological or spatial order. Chronological order arranges the details step-by-step in time order. Spatial order describes objects by their position in relation to each other. Either method is a good means of organizing a paragraph to provide coherence.

In a good paragraph the ideas should flow easily from one sentence to the next. Certain transitional devices are used to connect the sentences within a paragraph. Such transitional devices are linking expressions and phrases which act to connect ideas and to lead the reader to the next thought. Some of the most common linking expressions are included in the following list. A careful writer does not overuse any one expression.

first	in fact	so	along the same line
next	a case in point	thus	to conclude
then	an example of	also	last
therefore	and finally	however	more important

Unit 10 | **Language Elements in Review**

Complete these activities.

1.38 Write a paragraph defining the word *Christian.* Check your paragraph for the elements of a perfect paragraph to see if it fulfills all four requirements.

_____
_____
_____
_____
_____
_____

TEACHER CHECK _____ _____
                    initials   date

1.39 List three elements of a good paragraph.

a. _____
b. _____
c. _____

Answer these questions.

1.40 What is coherence?

_____
_____

1.41 What are two common ways of arranging information in paragraphs?

a. _____ b. _____

1.42 What purpose do linking expressions serve?

_____
_____
_____

Section 1 | **19**

LANGUAGE ELEMENTS IN REVIEW | Unit 10

LETTERS

Writing letters is a way people communicate with each other. Effective letter writing is a skill involving knowledge of writing techniques and knowledge of the different forms of letters. You studied these forms in Language Arts LIFEPAC 808.

Business letters. Three basic kinds of business letters are each written for a specific purpose. A letter of adjustment is usually written to a company when the customer has a problem. An order letter is written to a business requesting purchase of their product. A letter of application is a request for a job and an explanation of the writer's qualifications for that job.

The business letter form remains the same for each type of business letter. The parts of a business letter include the heading, the writer's address and the date; the inside address, the name and address of the company being

written; the salutation, or greeting; the body, the message of the letter; the closing, a phrase of ending; and the signature, which is the name of the writer.

A business letter in full block form should look like this example.

> 192 Elm Street
> Juneau, AK 99801
> August 5, 20_ _
>
> Brog's Record House
> 113 Main Street
> Capitol, WA 63021
>
> Gentlemen:
>
>   Please send me the current recording of *Gospel Singers for the Lord* by Barbara Jenkins.
>   I enclosed $18.95 to cover postage and handling.
>
> Sincerely yours,
>
> *John Whitehead*
>
> John Whitehead

| Business Letter Example

Personal letters. Three types of personal letters include the friendly, or informal letter; the invitation; and the thank-you note or letter. An informal letter is written to a friend and contains personal news and greetings. The invitation asks a person to attend a particular function or to join a group. The thank-you note is written in response to a gift or a friendly gesture.

The personal-letter form includes the heading, salutation, body, closing, and signature. The form of the personal letter remains the same for all types of informal writing. The personal letter should look like the example. The personal letter is usually written out by hand rather than typed.

Envelope. The form of an envelope remains the same for all types of letters. The address on an envelope remains the same for all types of letters. The address on an envelope should be distinctly written. A business letter envelope is usually typed. The envelope should have a return address and an address for the person who is to receive the letter.

A personal letter in full block form should look like this example.

> 7204 Vista Dr.
> Jacksonville, FL 32073
> February 21, 20_ _
>
> Dear Lizzie,
>
>   Thank you so much for the butterfly pin. It is beautiful on my new scarf. I'll write soon and tell you the latest news. Thanks again.
>
>   Love,
>
>   Anne

| Personal Letter Example

The envelope should look like this example.

Joshua Shaddock
613 147th Street
Overland Park, KS 66062

Mr. Phillip Roberts
Block Builders, Inc.
1111 Meadowbrook Lane
Waldorf, MD 20601

| Envelope Example

Answer these questions.

1.43   What are the three types of business letters?

   a. _____   b. _____   c. _____

1.44   What are the three types of personal letters?

   a. _____   b. _____   c. _____

Define or explain these terms.

1.45   greeting _____

1.46   closing _____

1.47   inside address _____

1.48   body _____

COMPOSITIONS

The composition, or essay, is an example of formal writing style. An essay is a group of related paragraphs written for a specific purpose. An essay is a written composition about one topic. Every detail in the essay should be closely related to the main topic.

The most difficult part of writing is merely getting started. Often, the purpose of a writing assignment is determined for you. Perhaps the teacher assigns a certain topic. If the assignment is general, then the writer must provide a good idea for a composition.

Choosing the subject is the first and most important part of essay writing. A wise student will choose a topic with which they are familiar about, or a topic for which they have strong feelings.

The next step in essay writing is to gather material for the paragraphs. Two good methods for gathering material include **brainstorming** and research. Brainstorming is appropriate if the essay will express an idea or opinion familiar to the writer. Research is necessary if the writing subject is unfamiliar and needs specific *documentation,* or proof.

Brainstorming is a technique for putting together what you know or think you know. The first step in brainstorming is to take pencil and paper and jot down all ideas that come into your head concerning a specific topic. Let's suppose that the assigned essay is titled "Why I Am a Christian." Brainstorming for that essay might look like this group of phrases or ideas.

> *believe in God / believe in Jesus as the Son of God / man should follow Bible teachings / man needs code for good / God is love / Jesus teaches man how to act for good / salvation is dependent on God's mercy and Christ's Crucifixion / parents taught me of God / belief in life after death / Christ is life's purpose / universe did not create itself...*

The thoughts do not follow any pattern other than being related to the general topic.

The next step would be to organize the thoughts in outline form, to expand the thoughts into sentence and paragraph form, and to write a rough draft for the essay. The brainstorming provides a focus for what the writer wants to write about.

Research is the second method of gathering information. Suppose the topic assigned is unfamiliar to the writer: "The Religion of the Early Arizona Settlers." The writer should write down a list of questions and should think of all possible resources for finding the answers. A library and the librarian provide good starting points.

Usually, the library staff are trained to help you find what is needed. You must know what you are looking for, however, before they can help you.

A good composition can be outlined.

   I. Thesis (one paragraph of introduction stating purpose)

   II. Body (two or more paragraphs of support and detail, depending on your essay)

   III. Conclusion (one paragraph)

The following checklist is an important guide for essay writing:

Composition Writing Checklist

1. Does the essay have a central idea? Is it clearly stated in the beginning, or thesis, paragraph?

2. Does the first statement catch the attention of your reader? It might (a) surprise, (b) question, (c) tell an anecdote, or a short story, or (d) state the purpose clearly and exactly. (Never start with "This paper will...")

3. Does each paragraph smoothly lead into the next?

4. Do you develop each point with anecdotes, examples, and comparisons? Do you back up all your opinions with facts?

5. Is the conclusion strong and in support of your thesis? Does the essay have a clincher statement that ties the essay together?

6. Are the sentences complete, grammatically correct, and correctly punctuated? Did you spell everything correctly?

Remember that you show who you are by the words that you choose. Words are a source of power because they can and should have an impact on your reader. If you try to make every word count in a positive way you will be a powerful writer.

Language Elements in Review | Unit 10

Answer these questions.

1.49 What is the most difficult part of essay writing? _____
_____

1.50 What are the five beginning steps for essay writing in order?

a. _____

b. _____

c. _____

d. _____

e. _____

1.51 What method of materials gathering should the writer use if the topic is unfamiliar?
_____

1.52 What method of materials gathering should the writer use for a topic they know well?
_____

Complete these activities.

1.53 Follow these steps to complete a composition on the topic "What Makes a Good Christian."

a. Brainstorm:

_____
_____
_____
_____
_____
_____
_____
_____
_____
_____
_____

b. Outline the notes from your brainstorming:

_____
_____
_____
_____
_____
_____
_____
_____
_____
_____
_____
_____

c. Expand the outline into sentence and paragraph form.

_____
_____
_____
_____
_____
_____
_____

d. Write the rough draft on a separate sheet of paper.
e. Check your rough draft with the checklist for composition writing.
f. Make changes in the essay where necessary and write your final copy on a separate sheet of paper.

TEACHER CHECK _____ _____
                                  initials   date

Language Elements in Review | Unit 10

SPELLING

Spelling Words-1 reviews words containing a combination of the letters *ei* or *ie*. You may remember the jingle from Language Arts LIFEPAC 801: "*i* before *e* except after *c*."

The combination *ie* usually is pronounced *ee*, but words such as *neighbor* and *weigh* are exceptions.

Spelling Words-1 (Review Words-801)

seize	height	resilient
surveillance	alien	receipt
heinous	conscience	sovereignty
medieval	convenience	siege
perceive	experience	freight
ceiling	mischievous	heirloom
believe	controversies	kaleidoscope
forfeit	subservient	lei
counterfeit		

Match the *ie/ei* words in the first column with the letter corresponding to the correct vowel sound. (Sounds may be used more than once.)

1.54 _____ seize   a. long *a*

1.55 _____ siege   b. long *e*

1.56 _____ lei   c. long *i*

1.57 _____ freight   d. short *e*

1.58 _____ height   e. short *i*

1.59 _____ ceiling

1.60 _____ heinous

1.61 _____ forfeit

1.62 _____ believe

1.63 _____ mischievous

1.64 _____ counterfeit

Unit 10 | **Language Elements in Review**

Play this game with a friend or helper.

1.65 Make a card out of construction paper or other heavy paper for each spelling word. Each person playing the game should have their own set of cards. Shuffle all the sets together and then deal each player cards until all are distributed. The players turn their cards face up at the same time. As each card is turned up, the player calls the vowel sound for their card aloud. If two or more players call out the same sound, the first player to cover all cards with their hand puts the pile of turned up cards in their "pot." The game is finished when all cards have been turned up. The winner is the player with the most cards in this "pot."

TEACHER CHECK _____ _____
                    initials date

This spelling review contains words that have homonyms and words that are commonly confused with similar forms. You may remember that homonyms are words that sound alike, but have different spellings and meanings. If you have difficulties with homonyms, refer to Language Arts LIFEPAC 805.

Spelling Words-1 (Review Words-805)

colonel	sleigh	complement
aisle	holy	counsel
whether	isle	except
corps	raze	weather
chord	wholly	affect
scent	personnel	altogether
reign	principal	racquet
neigh	already	ascent
niece		

Complete these activities.

1.66 Write homonyms for these spelling words.

a. colonel _____   b. aisle _____

c. corps _____   d. chord _____

e. scent _____   f. reign _____

Section 1 | 27

Language Elements in Review | Unit 10

g. niece _____ h. sleigh _____
i. holy _____ j. isle _____
k. raze _____ l. wholly _____
m. principal _____ n. already _____
o. complement _____ p. counsel _____
q. altogether _____ r. racquet _____
s. ascent _____ t. neigh _____

1.67 Write a sentence for each similar form.

a. whether _____
b. weather _____
c. except _____
d. accept _____
e. personnel _____
f. personal _____
g. affect _____
h. effect _____

ABC Ask a helper or your teacher to give you a practice spelling test of Spelling Words-1. Restudy the words you missed.

1.68 Review your spelling words in this section by using one or more of these devices. Ask your teacher which one(s) to complete.

a. Have a spelling bee type of competition with some of the members of your class.

b. Review with a friend.

c. Review with your parents.

d. Write each spelling word three times.

TEACHER CHECK _____ _____
                    initials   date

28 | Section 1

Unit 10 | **Language Elements in Review**

Review the material in this section in preparation for the Self Test. The Self Test will check your mastery of this particular section. The items missed on this Self Test will indicate specific areas where restudy is needed for mastery.

SELF TEST 1

Answer true or false (each answer, 1 point).

1.01 _____ In 1066 the Normans invaded England bringing French influence into England.

1.02 _____ Scientists have traced the English language to the parent language, Indo-European.

1.03 _____ The first dictionary published was written by Daniel Webster.

1.04 _____ All dictionaries are exactly the same.

1.05 _____ A thesaurus is a book of synonyms.

1.06 _____ Etymology is the study of insects.

1.07 _____ Abstract nouns are words that express ideas or qualities.

1.08 _____ A sentence does not always need a subject.

1.09 _____ A good writer can cover more than one topic in a paragraph.

1.010 _____ The thesis statement is the same as the essay title.

Match these items (each answer, 2 points).

1.011 _____ sentence   a. generating ideas
1.012 _____ paragraph   b. group of words
1.013 _____ composition   c. gathering unfamiliar information
1.014 _____ brainstorming   d. group of paragraphs
1.015 _____ research   e. scientists who study language
1.016 _____ dialects   f. story or tale
1.017 _____ anecdote   g. group of sentences
1.018 _____ fragment   h. two or more sentences incorrectly combined by the excessive use of *and* and *so*
1.019 _____ run-on   i. common linking expressions
1.020 _____ first, next, then j. part of a sentence
                                   k. local characteristics of speech

Section 1 | 29

Language Elements in Review | Unit 10

Name the part of speech for the word in italics (each answer, 3 points).

1.021 _____ Theresa *walked* and *talked* like a clown.

1.022 _____ *Many* people believe in God.

1.023 _____ *Children* should be seen and not heard.

1.024 _____ *I* am the way, the truth, and the life.

1.025 _____ *Quickly*, lead the way to the attic.

1.026 _____ The children were pleased with *themselves*.

1.027 _____ *Who* is the leader of this group?

1.028 _____ Our *minister* is an excellent speaker.

Define these words (each answer, 4 points).

1.029 noun _____

1.030 verb _____

1.031 pronoun _____

1.032 adjective _____

1.033 adverb _____

Answer these questions (each answer, 5 points).

1.034 What is an acronym? _____

_____

1.035 What is etymology? _____

_____

1.036 Who introduced the first United States dictionary? _____

1.037 What are the two basic parts of a sentence?

a. _____ b. _____

75 / 94   SCORE _____   TEACHER _____ _____
                                          initials   date

ABC Take your spelling test of Spelling Words-1.

Unit 10 | **Language Elements in Review**

2. COMMUNICATION

Communication is a complicated process. We communicate effectively when our audience understands the message we are trying to **convey**. The ability to communicate is one of the most important parts of being human.

Communication may take the form either of nonverbal communication or of verbal communication. In this section you will review both categories of communication.

You will study the elements of nonverbal messages—how to use gestures, facial expressions, and pantomime to communicate. You will reconsider the guidelines for oral expression and will review the suggestions for being a good listener. You will also restudy the spelling words from Language Arts LIFEPACs 804 through 806.

SECTION OBJECTIVES

Review these objectives. When you have completed this section, you should be able to:

12. List three unspoken factors of communication.
13. Name three basic purposes of speeches.
14. Correctly identify word parts as prefix, suffix, or root.
15. Explain ways to unlock word meanings.
16. Identify a statement as fact or opinion.
21. Spell the review words correctly.

VOCABULARY

Study these words to enhance your learning success in this section.

convey (kun vā´). Express, put across.
grimace (gri mās´). A twisting of the face expressing pain, contempt, or disgust.
involuntary (in vol´ un ter ē). Not performed willingly.
monotone (mon´ u tōn). Manner of speaking, singing, and so forth without change of pitch.

UNSPOKEN FACTORS IN COMMUNICATION

Nonverbal communication is used to express attitude, mood, and intention. A person may use gestures and facial expressions with speech to *add* to the message of the words, or they may use gestures, facial expressions, and pantomime in place of words.

If a person tells you, "You're a real pal," you would interpret these words by their literal meaning as a friendly compliment. Now imagine a person speaking the words "You're a real pal" with their hands on their hips and an angry facial expression. The meaning suddenly shifted from a friendly compliment to a sarcastic remark.

Language Elements in Review | Unit 10

| "You're a real pal!"

Complete these activities.

2.1 List three types of nonverbal communication.

a. _____ b. _____

c. _____

2.2 Define these words. Use the dictionary, if necessary.

a. literal _____

b. pantomime _____

2.3 Say the word *yes* quietly to a classmate showing the following meanings: complete agreement, anger, curiosity, eagerness to hear more, impatience, and doubt.

a. Write some the nonverbal ways you expressed the different meanings.

_____

_____

b. Have your teacher write any nonverbal actions you may not have been aware of using.

_____

_____

TEACHER CHECK _____ _____
                  initials   date

32 | Section 2

Facial Expressions. Have you ever watched a baby communicate? Before a child ever says the word "mama," they are able to express themselves with a smile. The face is probably the most important indicator of nonverbal messages. Eyes, nose, mouth, and facial muscles work together to send meaning. An entire language of face is learned right along with spoken language.

Many facial expressions are **involuntary**. A speaker can go through an entire vocabulary of facial expressions without ever being aware of any shift in position. Only a conscious effort to control facial expressions will bring a full awareness of how much people rely on facial tools of communication. Facial expressions display emotions, moods, and attitudes. Often facial expressions can completely change the meaning of words.

A variety of facial expressions are part of the nonverbal vocabulary. The mouth can smile, frown, pucker, purse, pout, fall open, and **grimace**. The nose can wrinkle, twitch, sniff, and sneer. The eyes can wink, blink, flutter, gaze directly, stare, widen, squint, and shut completely. Eyebrows raise and lower to different levels with various degrees of meaning. Each expression has its own meaning and expresses a specific emotion, mood, or attitude.

Answer these questions.

2.4 What is the most important indicator of nonverbal messages?
_____

2.5 What are the expressive components of the face?
_____

2.6 What expressions can the mouth make?
_____
_____

2.7 What expressions can the eyes make?
_____
_____

2.8 What expressions can the nose make?
_____

Complete this activity.

2.9 Use a mirror to watch yourself as you try all the expressions you have previously listed. Look up any words you do not understand so that you are sure of the meaning you are to express.

Language Elements in Review | Unit 10

Gestures. Many gestures are universal in meaning. Gestures include any movement of the body, especially the hands, to express a thought. Though some gestures differ in meaning from country to country, many gestures can be understood anywhere.

The origin of most of the gestures that are common to us is difficult to trace.

The following list contains several common gestures and their usual meanings:

Gesture	Meaning
shaking hands	friendship
rubbing hands together	anticipation
placing palms together	prayer, supplication
raising the hand	asking for recognition
beckoning	come
thumbs up	approval
patting back	encouragement
palms up	don't have, don't know
shaking fist	anger
clapping	approval
making the sign of the cross	religious
wringing the hands	despair
pointing	look (go) there
rubbing stomach	hunger
rubbing head	puzzlement
fist in palm	threatening
spreading hands	blessing

Answer these questions.

2.10 What gesture might Jesus have used when He chased the money changers from the Temple? _____

2.11 What gesture might Jesus have used, after John baptized Him, in speaking to Satan and saying "Get thee behind me, Satan"? _____

2.12 What gesture might Jesus have used in saying "Lazarus, come forth"? _____

Complete this activity.

2.13 Look up the following Scripture references concerning gestures Jesus used. Try to picture the gestures in your mind as you read the Bible. Describe His gestures. Luke 24:50 and 51

_____

_____

LANGUAGE ARTS 810

LIFEPAC TEST

NAME _____

DATE _____

SCORE _____

LANGUAGE ARTS 810: LIFEPAC TEST

Match these items (each answer, 2 points).

1. _____ morpheme
2. _____ brainstorming
3. _____ coherence
4. _____ sequence
5. _____ composition
6. _____ formal essay
7. _____ fact
8. _____ lead
9. _____ thesaurus
10. _____ proper nouns

a. beginning sentence of a news article
b. can be proved
c. the smallest meaningful unit of the English language
d. generating ideas
e. order of occurrence
f. should be capitalized
g. logic, clarity
h. serious writing
i. provides synonyms
j. group of paragraphs
k. convey

Answer *true* or *false* (each answer, 1 point).

11. _____ The parent language of English is Indo-European.
12. _____ Abstract nouns should always be capitalized.
13. _____ Always spell out numbers when you use them in sentences.
14. _____ Acronyms are not punctuated in the way abbreviations are.
15. _____ A comma splice is an incomplete sentence.
16. _____ A letter of adjustment usually concerns a problem with a skill or a product.
17. _____ *Ex* is a prefix.
18. _____ Context clues are helpful in unlocking word meanings.
19. _____ A news article should always be based on opinion.
20. _____ An essay must have multiple paragraphs.

Unit 810 | Language Arts

Answer these questions (each answer, 5 points).

21. What is the difference between fact and opinion?
_____
_____
_____
_____
_____

22. What valuable information can be found in a dictionary?
_____
_____
_____
_____

23. Who wrote the first United States dictionary in 1806? _____

24. What are the four elements of the "perfect paragraph"?

　　a. _____
　　b. _____
　　c. _____
　　d. _____

Write *F* for fact, *O* for opinion (each answer, 3 points).

25. _____ The boys in our class are smarter than the girls.
26. _____ Amy has blue eyes.
27. _____ John has beautiful hair.
28. _____ The preacher lives on Alton Street.

Punctuate and capitalize these sentences (each mark, 1 point).

29　　her sister in law is editor in chief of the local paper

30.　　help me Joan cried im falling

31.　　can you see george mary or fred coming

LIFEPAC TEST | 3

Language Arts | Unit 810

Complete these statements (each answer, 3 points).

32. Noah Webster wrote the first United States a. _____ in the year b. _____ .

33. The book of synonyms most commonly used is called _____ .

34. Three main purposes for speeches include a. _____ , b. _____ , and c. _____ .

35. Two main classifications of types of communication include a. _____ and b. _____ .

Define these terms (each answer, 4 points).

36. autobiography _____
    _____
    _____

37. nonverbal communication _____
    _____
    _____

ABC Take your LIFEPAC Spelling Test.

Pantomime. Pantomime or "mime" is the art of total non-verbal communication. A person or an actor uses gestures and facial expressions to communicate. Movements and gestures are exaggerated a great deal. Entire stories can be told by the effective use of pantomime.

Marcel Marceau is one of the most famous of the pantomime artists. He has developed his performance to near perfection. The make-up he uses has become a standard in pantomime performances. The actor usually wears black clothing or leotards. The face is painted with a white base, and the basic features of the face are outlined in black. The outlining helps to exaggerate the facial expressions allowing the actor's features to be seen clearly.

Pantomime requires a great deal of the actor. They perform on a bare stage with very simple props.

The acting is a series of make-believe motions very similar to the motions used in a game of charades. If the artist performs well, the audience will believe in what the actor is doing.

A pantomimist must be able to express emotions and feelings clearly. Posture, facial expressions, gestures, and style of walking are all skills for the pantomime actor to master. Effective pantomime takes hours of practice.

The actor must be aware of their imaginary setting. If the actor is miming baking a cake, they must picture the size of the imaginary spoon.

| "The make-up of the pantomime artist is designed to help exaggerate the facial features and to create a more expressive face."

If they set a make-believe bowl on the table, they must pick up the same size bowl from the same spot later. Communication of ideas through pantomime is a difficult skill to master.

People use pantomime every day to increase the effectiveness of their communication. The policeman controlling traffic must rely on pantomime to regulate the flow of cars. A referee depends on a pantomime vocabulary to direct a game. The military uses its own design of nonverbal signals. Sign language allows deaf people to communicate easily. All people use forms of pantomime at times to express themselves clearly.

Complete these statements.

2.14 Three basic things a pantomime actor uses to communicate are

a. _____ b. _____ , and c. _____ .

2.15 Some of the daily uses of pantomime include a. _____ ,

b. _____ , c. _____ ,

and d. _____ .

Complete this activity.

2.16 Choose one of the following suggestions and "perform" in pantomime for a friend. Your pantomime should tell a story. See if your friend can interpret your story correctly.

Walking a very large dog
An overworked robot
A rebellious puppet
A small child with a large ice cream cone
A newly-hired pizza maker

TEACHER CHECK

_____ _____
initials   date

SPOKEN FACTORS OF COMMUNICATION

Spoken language reveals much information about the speaker. A person's speech can indicate where they have lived, how much education they have had, and what kind of person they are. Many standards are set for speaking. Some deal with grammar, others with voice tone. One standard for speech with which all Christians should be familiar is the Bible. The Bible encourages people to express themselves wisely and well, to speak kindly.

Speaking qualities. An effective speaker can hold the interest of the audience and can make them understand the message. Each person has their own speaking patterns which are formed by their personality and interactions or observations with others. Children learn to speak by the example of their parents, teachers, and friends, as well as by exposure to other individuals in a variety of settings. As Christians we should model our speech patterns after the best example available. We must make an effort to choose our speaking qualities so that our speech is a glory to God.

A good speaker will not speak until they have a clear understanding of the topic. Familiarity with the subject is quite important and often calls for a good deal of work. The first step of any formal speech is the gathering of information. A speaker should research for facts and plan the speech so that the information is presented logically and clearly.

The basic types of formal speeches are presented for three purposes: to inform, to persuade, and to entertain. A teacher lectures to inform students about a certain subject. The minister speaks to persuade their congregation to follow Christ. A comedian speaks to entertain the audience. All three types of speech require that the speaker be familiar with the subject and that they plan ahead to be well-prepared.

A speech is made more effective if the speaker uses appropriate nonverbal aids. Gestures, facial expressions, and posture are important parts of a speech. These nonverbal aids show the audience the attitude the speaker has toward the subject. Enthusiasm for the topic is the most effective means of keeping the attention of the audience. Such enthusiasm can only be communicated through nonverbal aids and tone of voice.

A good speaker will have a clear outline to guide the presentation. Their notes are clear and brief so that the speaker does not "read" to the audience. Many speakers write key ideas or words on note cards and rehearse the speech in front of a mirror using only the notes on the cards. The note-card method will assure the speaker that they know the speech well enough to talk to the audience rather than to read to them. A speaker often practices the use of appropriate gestures, good posture, and eye-contact as they rehearse the speech. A clear and pleasant voice is easier to listen to than a loud, shrill tone. A speaker should aim their voice toward the person in the last row and should speak with slow, clear syllables. They should raise their voice to emphasize an idea, to restate a thought, or to make a strong point. In order to avoid a **monotone** voice, a speaker should practice in front of a friend or relative in order to get feedback and become comfortable with expression.

Answer true or false.

2.17 _____ Each person has their own speaking patterns.

2.18 _____ Children pick up certain speech habits from people they hear most often.

2.19 _____ A good speaker can make a speech without preparing for it.

2.20 _____ The first step in making a speech is to organize it logically.

Complete these statements.

2.21 Three basic purposes for making a formal speech are a. _____ ,

b. _____ , and c. _____ .

2.22 Planning a speech helps the information to be presented in a

a. _____ , and b. _____ way.

2.23 Three nonverbal aids that can make a speech more effective are

a. _____ , b. _____ , and c. _____ .

Speech organization. In Language Arts LIFEPAC 809 you studied the *pentad,* which is a five-part device for organizing a speech or an oral report. The pentad should cover the following areas.

- What action (what?)
- What agent (who?)
- What setting (where? and when?)
- What means (how?)
- What purpose (why?)

As you organize your speech, be sure to answer each of the questions of the pentad. Whatever type of speech you prepare, you should include a *thesis* to guide your organization. The rest of your speech should support, prove, or carry out the purpose or direction indicated by the thesis.

Biblical standards. In First Peter 4:11 Christians are instructed about the manner in which they should speak. "If any man speak, let him speak as the oracles of God; if any man minister, let him do it as of the ability which God giveth; that God in all things may be glorified through Jesus Christ: to whom be praise and dominion for ever and ever. Amen." What better goal for a Christian than to try to spread God's praise and glory. To be able to "spread the Gospel to every creature," we must be able to express ourselves to every creature. We must be able to speak so that others will understand the message we want to **convey**.

Complete this activity.

2.24 Check your Bible for descriptions of the manner in which Jesus spoke. Write down at least three Biblical references.

a. _____

_____

b. _____

_____

c. _____

_____

Complete these activities.

2.25 Interview a friend. Prepare an outline and note cards. Plan a speech to introduce that friend to your teacher or a helper. You may want to use the following questions for a guide in your interview.

a. What is your name?

b. Where have you lived or traveled?

c. What is your relationship with Christ?

d. What is one word that describes you?

e. Have you any hobbies? Pets?

f. Describe your family.

g. What is the biggest problem facing our country today?

h. What are your plans for your future?

TEACHER CHECK _____ _____
initials   date

2.26 List the questions the pentad should answer.

a. _____

b. _____

c. _____

d. _____

e. _____

COMPREHENDING COMMUNICATION

To communicate with another person involves more than getting your message to him. Also important is the ability to understand what the other person has to say. Communication only takes place when people understand each other.

Following directions. People are asked to follow directions every day. Teachers give instructions for class assignments. Road signs and signals instruct drivers about certain rules and conditions. A boss explains a task to an employee. A person who applies for a job must complete an application form. People must register to vote or to license their cars. A cook follows a recipe. A boy tries to build a model airplane. All these situations involve following written or oral directions.

Listening. The ability to listen is a difficult skill to master. The listener must concentrate on the words spoken and remember what was said. The listener must follow the *sequence* of the directions so that the instructions can be followed step by step.

A common situation for listening to oral instructions involves a telephone conversation. The ability to comprehend what the person on the phone is trying to communicate is a difficult task. The listener must rely entirely on what they hear because a telephone cannot convey nonverbal signals. A person should listen closely and repeat the directions given so that they remember the steps and the order in which the directions were given.

Written directions can be very hard to understand. One advantage to written directions is that the reader can overlook the instructions until each step is clearly understood. They should make a mental note of each step while reading the directions. A person should follow instructions one at a time until the task is complete.

Complete these activities.

2.27 Ask two people to read the following dialogue aloud. Write a phone message on the lines below the dialogue when they have finished reading. Do not look back at the dialogue as you write.

John: Hello.

Mary: Hello, this is Mary Worthington. Is Alice at home?

John: No. Alice is at the store. She'll be back at four o'clock.

Mary: Oh dear. I need to speak to her. It's important!

John: Can I give her a message for you?

Mary: Yes. Please tell her I called. I will pick her up for choir practice early because my brother needs the car. She will have to be ready twenty minutes before the time I told her before. Will you tell her that?

John: Sure. I'll tell her. Good-bye.

Mary: Good-bye, John. Thank you.

Message: _____
_____
_____
_____
_____

2.28 Now go back and check the dialogue. Be sure you have the important information in your message. Answer the following questions:

a. Who is the message for? _____

b. Who is the message from? _____

c. What is the message about? _____
_____
_____

TEACHER CHECK _____ _____
                    initials   date

2.29 Follow these instructions step by step. You will need a pencil and a ruler.

Measure the sides of the square.

Make a straight line from the middle of the bottom of the square to the middle of the top of the square.

Measure half way up the left side of the square.

Make a dot halfway up the left side of the square.

Measure half way up the right side of the square.

Make a dot half way up the right side of the square.

Join the two dots with a straight line.

2.30 Now answer these questions.

a. What are the measurements of the square? _____

b. What is the symbol you drew in the square? _____

Unit 10 | Language Elements in Review

SPELLING

The spelling words in this review are commonly misspelled words in our language. These tricky words are taken from Language Arts LIFEPACs 801 through 809.

Spelling Words-2 (Review Words-1)

reference	conference	annihilate
omitting	burglary	calendar
Christianity	tentative	imperative
picnicker	prerogative	restaurant
recurring	laboratory	Wednesday
involuntary	irrelevant	kidnapped
interrupt	guarantee	thoroughly
deceit	acknowledge	opportunity
separate		

Complete these activities.

2.31 Alphabetize Review Words-1.

a. _____ b. _____

c. _____ d. _____

e. _____ f. _____

g. _____ h. _____

i. _____ j. _____

k. _____ l. _____

m. _____ n. _____

o. _____ p. _____

q. _____ r. _____

s. _____ t. _____

u. _____ v. _____

w. _____ x. _____

y. _____

Language Elements in Review | Unit 10

The spelling words from this review have like-sounding endings, or suffixes. The ending are *-ent* or *-ant*, *-ible* or *-able*. These spelling words were also taken from Language Arts LIFEPACs 801 through 809.

Spelling Words-2 (Review Words-2)

covenant	significant	lovable
confident	amiable	lieutenant
elegant	permissible	obedient
hesitant	excusable	irrelevant
somnolent	infallible	extravagant
supplement	unstable	unpleasant
desirable	accessible	pre-existent
vigilant	responsible	efficient
pertinent		

Write your spelling words under the correct suffix in alphabetical order.

2.32 -ible

a. _____
b. _____
c. _____
d. _____

2.33 -able

a. _____
b. _____
c. _____
d. _____
e. _____

2.34 -ent

a. _____
b. _____
c. _____
d. _____
e. _____
f. _____
g. _____

2.35 -ant

a. _____
b. _____
c. _____
d. _____
e. _____
f. _____
g. _____
h. _____
i. _____

Look at these activities.

2.36   Review your spelling words in this section by using one or more of these devices. Ask your teacher which one(s) to complete.

   a. Have a spelling bee type of competition with some of the members of your class.

   b. Review with a friend.

   c. Review with your parents.

   d. Write each spelling word three times.

TEACHER CHECK _____ _____
                   initials   date

Ask your teacher to give you a practice spelling test of Spelling Words-2. Restudy the words you missed.

Review the material in this section in preparation for the Self Test. The Self Test will check your mastery of this particular section as well as your knowledge of the previous section. The items missed on this Self Test will indicate specific areas where restudy is needed for mastery.

Section 2 | **43**

SELF TEST 2

Answer true or false (each answer, 1 point).

2.01 _____ Gesture is one factor of unspoken communication.

2.02 _____ A gesture can completely change the meaning of common words and phrases.

2.03 _____ Our nonverbal vocabulary includes all our facial expressions.

2.04 _____ A sentence always needs a predicate.

2.05 _____ An essay is a group of paragraphs.

2.06 _____ Many facial expressions are involuntary.

2.07 _____ Pantomime is totally nonverbal communication.

2.08 _____ Mime artists use many props to tell their stories.

2.09 _____ A good speaker does not read to the audience.

2.010 _____ A monotone is important in oral expression.

Match these items (each answer, 2 points).

2.011 _____ coherence
2.012 _____ so, also, therefore
2.013 _____ grimace
2.014 _____ pout
2.015 _____ salutation
2.016 _____ etymology
2.017 _____ adjustment
2.018 _____ brainstorming
2.019 _____ posture
2.020 _____ shaking hands

a. the greeting of a letter
b. word showing relationship between two nouns
c. linking expressions
d. a type of business letter
e. contortion of face showing pain
f. logic, order
g. study of word history
h. facial expression using mouth
i. common gesture of friendship
j. way of holding the body
k. a way to come up with ideas

Unit 10 | **Language Elements in Review**

Complete these statements (each answer, 3 points).

2.021 The three unspoken factors of communication are a. _____ ,
b. _____ , and c. _____ .

2.022 The three basic categories or purposes of speeches are to a. _____ ,
to b. _____ , and to c. _____ .

2.023 A good speaker should aim their voice _____
_____ .

2.024 Two basic goals of a Christian in speaking are a. _____
_____ and
b. _____ .

2.025 Two main categories of communication are a. _____ and
b. _____ .

2.026 Two word books which are necessary to the good writer are the
a. _____ and the b. _____ .

Complete these items (each answer, 3 points).

2.027 List the outline form of the essay.

a. _____

b. _____

c. _____

2.028 List the elements of a perfect paragraph.

a. _____

b. _____

c. _____

d. _____

Answer these questions (each answer, 5 points).

2.029 What are similarities between the characteristics of a paragraph and an essay?

_____
_____
_____

Section 2 | **45**

Language Elements in Review | Unit 10

2.030 What purpose do linking expressions serve?

Punctuate and capitalize these paragraphs (each mark, 1 point).

2.031 one day my family and i decided to go on a picnic mother packed fried chicken and a big chocolate cake my sister in law brought some potato salad and twenty cans of cola dad hooked our boat to the camper and we were on our way

Rodney my brother unloaded their supplies, and i helped mom spread out all our food just as i was helping myself to lindas potato salad it started raining

Quick mother shouted get the food inside

we finished the rest of the meal inside our tiny camper doesnt that sound like a fun picnic

110 / 138   SCORE _____   TEACHER _____ _____
                                      initials   date

ABC Take your spelling test of Spelling Words-2.

46 | Section 2

Unit 10 | **Language Elements in Review**

3. READING

The ability to read well and to understand literature will bring lifelong pleasure and will provide a tool for learning and for exploring any interest. In this section you will review the basic reading and literature skills you have studied in the Language Arts LIFEPAC 800 series.
You will explore word parts and their meanings. You will study ways to unlock word meanings: context, sequence, and analogy. You will look at nonfiction forms of literature such as news articles, essays, and autobiographies. You will also review the spelling words from Language Arts LIFEPACs 800 series.

SECTION OBJECTIVES

Review these objectives. When you have completed this section, you should be able to:

14. Correctly identify word parts as prefix, suffix, or root.
15. Explain ways to unlock word meanings.
16. Identify a statement as fact or opinion.
17. Explain sequence.
18. State the main purpose of a news article.
19. State the main purpose of an essay.
20. List three elements of autobiography.
21. Spell the review words correctly.

VOCABULARY

Study these words to enhance your learning success in this section.

affix (u fiks´). A syllable or syllables added to a base or root word to change its meaning; a prefix or suffix.

chronological (kron u loj´ u kul). Time order; arranged in order of occurrence.

lead (lēd). The first sentence in a news article.

morpheme (môr´ fēm). The smallest part of a word that has meaning of its own.

precise (pri sīs´). Exact.

sequence (sē´ kwuns). Order of occurrence.

Section 3 | 47

LANGUAGE ELEMENTS IN REVIEW | Unit 10

WORD PARTS

A word is made up of many meaningful parts. The smallest meaningful unit in our language is called a **morpheme**. Words are made by joining morphemes. Morphemes are root words, prefixes, suffixes, and inflections. Two classifications of morphemes are *free morphemes* (the unit which can be used alone as a word having a distinct meaning); and *bound morphemes* (a unit which must be used with a root word to affect the meaning of that word). A bound morpheme has no meaning of its own and must be used with another word part.

A *prefix* is a morpheme added to the beginning of a root word. Common prefixes include *pre-, in-, un-, inter-, dis-,* and *bi-*. *Suffixes* are morphemes added to the end of a root. Common suffix endings include *-tion* and *-ment*.

An inflection is a special type of morpheme that changes the grammatical function of the word. Examples of the inflection morpheme include *-d, -ed, -t, -s, -es, -ing, -er, -est*, and *'s or s'*. The three morpheme types—prefixes, suffixes, and inflections—are called **affixes**.

A root word, or base word, is the word unit which supplies the basic meaning. Basic meaning is changed or expanded when affixes are joined to the root word. Roots are not always easy to recognize. Adding a suffix or inflection often makes changing the spelling of the root word necessary for simple pronunciation. Imagine the root *horror* plus the suffix *-ible* without any change in the root word—*horrorible*. If you have forgotten some of these words and word parts, go back to Language Arts LIFEPAC 801.

Complete these activities.

3.1 Underline the prefix or suffix in these words. Use a dictionary if necessary. Some words have more than one affix.

a. unnecessary   b. incomplete   c. pretest
d. disbelieve   e. hopelessness   f. rejection
g. baptism   h. precious   i. discourage
j. athletic   k. Christian   l. lifelike
m. silliness   n. beautiful   o. undercoating

3.2 Underline the root word. Write the correct spelling without affixes on the line.

a. holiness   _____
b. depth   _____
c. miraculous   _____
d. sensible   _____
e. happiness   _____

Unit 10 | **Language Elements in Review**

3.3 Take a morpheme from the affix column and add a morpheme from the root column. Combine the two morphemes to make a word in the third column. There are multiple ways to combine the morphemes. Check your spelling in a dictionary.

affix	root	word	affix	root	word
ing	solve	resolve	in	repeat	f. _____
pre	love	a. _____	bi	glued	g. _____
re	sight	b. _____	less	help	h. _____
dis	reason	c. _____	ed	sift	i. _____
tion	own	d. _____	ist	annual	j. _____
ment	content	e. _____		psalm	k. _____

3.4 Define *morpheme*. _____

_____

CONTEXT CLUES

What do you do when you come to a new word in your reading? If you are reading an assignment or are trying to master a subject, you probably will take the time to check a dictionary or glossary for the exact word meaning. If you are reading for pleasure, you may not wish to take the time to find a **precise** meaning. You may guess at the word meaning or even skip over the word. Reading over, or skipping the word, is not a good reading technique. Ways to look for clues in your reading will act like keys to unlock word meanings for you.

Context clues are one good way of figuring out new word meanings. The reader becomes a detective and looks for hints from the way the word is used. Have you ever heard a politician say "I was quoted out of context"? What they are saying is that the meaning of their message was changed when reporters left out some of the words or important information.

Picture the following situation: A young boy goes home and tells his mother, "The teacher says that I am doing really well in school." The mother is pleased and appreciative. When parent-teacher conferences take place, the mother expects to hear praise and good reports. She is amazed to hear the boy's teacher say that he is not doing well at all. The mother says, "My son told me you said he is doing really well in school." The teacher is amazed. "What I told your son," the teacher says, "was that he does very well in school *when he pays attention*." The boy had taken the teacher's words out of context.

To determine the meaning of a word using context clues, the good reading detective will look at the whole sentence around the word. They will look at *the way* the word is used, *the part* of speech, *the whole idea* of the sentence, and *the location* of the word in the sentence. All these clues work together to point the way to solving the meaning of the new word.

Section 3 | 49

Language Elements in Review | Unit 10

Using context clues, guess at the meaning of the nonsense words in these sentences.
Write the part of speech each word represents.

3.5 I watched the falling *gorp* get the ground all wet this morning.

a. part of speech _____ b. probable meaning _____

3.6 Jane *gorped* over the fence to cross the field.

a. part of speech _____ b. probable meaning _____

3.7 This *gorp* day really makes me feel depressed.

a. part of speech _____ b. probable meaning _____

Using context clues, guess at the meaning of the word in italics.
Check your answers in a dictionary to see how close you are to being right.

3.8 The minister offered a *fervent* prayer for the children who were kidnapped.
_____

3.9 Until the final game, our football team had seemed *invincible*. _____

3.10 The members of the school board do not expect any *remuneration* for their services.
_____

3.11 Alcohol has a *pernicious* effect on the human body. _____

SEQUENCE

The **sequence** is the order in which several items, events, or ideas are arranged or presented. If you note sequence of events as you read, you will be able to understand new words and ideas. Sequence is especially important in understanding directions or instructions. The ability to arrange what you read into a logical pattern will help you to be a good reading detective.

Chronological order. Sequence can be in **chronological**, or time, order. Chronological order can be a list, or series, of steps or events. To establish chronological sequence, the reader must ask, "Which comes first?" The answer to that question is the beginning of establishing chronological sequence.

Spatial order. Spatial order is achieved when the writer records what they see. The writer uses logical progression from one detail to the next in a scene or area that they are describing. Spatial order keeps unity by describing objects as they relate to each other.

Other order. The sequence of describing the particular to the general includes specific statements that lead to a more general conclusion. The sequence can be reversed so that the writer begins with a general statement and develops the information toward proving a particular statement.

Unit 10 | Language Elements in Review

Write these sets of words in a logical sequence.

3.12 teenager, grandpa, toddler, infant, father

a. _____ b. _____

c. _____ d. _____

e. _____

3.13 Mark, John, Matthew, Acts, Luke

a. _____ b. _____

c. _____ d. _____

e. _____

3.14 set the date, mail the invitations, decide to have a party, stamp the invitations, make a guest list

a. _____ b. _____

c. _____ d. _____

e. _____

FACT AND OPINION

Another important reading skill is the ability to decide if statements are *facts* or *opinions*. You know that you must not believe everything you read. Knowing the difference between fact and opinion may mean knowing whether to believe what you read.

In deciding whether a statement is fact or opinion, a student should consider the author of the statement. Take a look at what the author's intentions are in making the statement. If the author is attempting to persuade the reader of something, look very closely at their words. In general, a fact is something that can be proved. An opinion is something that can be believed, but it lacks actual evidence to support it.

Section 3 | 51

Complete these activities.

3.15 Write *F* next to factual statements. Write *O* next to opinions.

a. _____ Mary's eyes are blue.

b. _____ Alicia walked into class after the bell rang.

c. _____ Don is the best student in the class.

d. _____ The Bible teaches Christians about God's love.

e. _____ Apple pie is better than chocolate cake.

3.16 Play "Fact or Opinion."

Make two small signs—a *fact* sign and an *opinion* sign for each player. Use a colored marker or colored poster paper for the signs (green for fact, red for opinion). Select one person to write down fifteen to twenty statements—some facts, some opinions. This person will read one statement. The other players will use their signs to indicate which fits the statement. The first player using the correct sign is given twenty-five points. The player who scores 100 points wins the round.

NEWS ARTICLES

Americans gather a major part of their information from reading the newspaper. The newspaper is a source of knowledge for current events, world news, local occurrences, and general public information. Because journalism is such an important source of information, you need to know what to look for in a good news article.

A good news article is a factual representation of an issue, problem, or event. The news article should be written clearly and simply. The author's opinion cannot be included in a news article. All opinion should be found on the editorial page only. A news article should consist of facts.

A good news article should give the total story, answering these questions: *Who, What, When, Why, Where,* and *How?* Most articles will be written with one or more of the questions (called the 5 W's plus H) in the **lead** or beginning sentence.

News articles are written in what is known as *inverted pyramid* style. The most important information is found in the very beginning paragraphs. Each paragraph in the sequence should contain less and less important information.

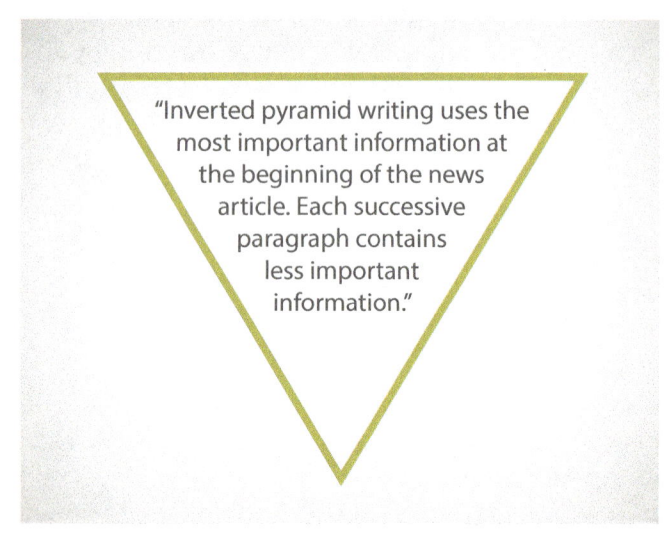

"Inverted pyramid writing uses the most important information at the beginning of the news article. Each successive paragraph contains less important information."

| Inverted pyramid

Newspapers are like puzzles. They must be put together so that everything fits into columns. An editor will often cut the end paragraphs from an article to make it fit the space allowed. For this reason, the inverted pyramid writing style is necessary.

The main information of the story can be gathered from reading the first paragraph. Each successive paragraph adds details. The lead sentence should tell the reader the most important part of the story. It should catch the attention of the reader without being "sensational" or misleading.

Complete these activities.

3.17 Read the following news story and answer the questions about it.

Jane Taylor was married at the First Christian Church in Williams, Virginia, on Saturday, November 15. The bride is the daughter of the prominent judge, the Honorable Albert Taylor. Miss Taylor was joined in holy matrimony to Robert Farsdale II, also from Williams.

The couple will make their home in Williams after an extended European tour. The bride is a graduate of Barksdale University where she graduated with full honors.

The groom is currently employed by Los Arcos del Oro. He is a graduate of Williams High School.

The ceremony took place at 8 o'clock in the evening. Attendants for the bride were her three sisters, Julia, Joanne, and Jill. The bridal gown was of ivory silk with a seed pearl bodice while the brides-maids' gowns were of pink satin and lace. Each carried pink and white rosebuds.

Attending the ceremony were the bride's father and grandmother, Mrs. Eldea Taylor, from California.

a. What questions does the lead answer in this article?

_____   _____   _____   _____

b. Is the article factual? _____

c. What is the least important information?

_____

_____

_____

LANGUAGE ELEMENTS IN REVIEW | Unit 10

3.18 Find a news story in a newspaper, magazine, or online source. Notice the way each of the following questions are answered and indicate the part of the story in which each is located.

a. Who is the story about? _____

b. Where did the story take place? _____

c. When did the story take place? _____

d. Exactly what happened? _____

e. How did it happen? _____

_____

Exchange news stories and answers with a friend.

TEACHER CHECK _____ _____
initials   date

3.19 Using the information given, write catchy and specific lead sentences for possible news articles.

a. A woman had quintuplets. Her name is Alba Robertsive. She is 49 years old. They were born at John C. Washington Hospital. They were born at 3 o'clock on Saturday, January 5. She is the wife of the mayor of the city. John C. Washington Hospital is in Norfolk, Virginia. The Robertsives live is Bethseda, Maryland. Alan Robertsive dislikes flowers.

_____
_____

b. A picnic is going to take place. The picnic is sponsored by the Myville Community Club. The picnic will be held in the pasture by Jay's Barn. It will be on Saturday, May 5, at noon. Tickets can be purchased. Admission is $1.50 per person. The picnic will be a benefit. Proceeds from ticket sales will go to the Myville Children's Home.

_____
_____

3.20 Choose one of the preceding sets of information and write a news article. Then answer the questions.

a. Did you use inverted pyramid style? _____

b. Take out your last paragraph. Does your article still make sense and tell the story? _____

TEACHER CHECK _____ _____
initials   date

54 | Section 3

ESSAYS

The essay is a specific type of literary prose. The function of essay writing is usually expository, or to explain something about a certain limited topic. The essay is usually short and is classified as nonfiction.

Two essay types include the *formal essay* and the *informal essay*. The formal essay is serious in tone and subject. The main purpose of the formal essay is to inform by means of a logical, organized style. The informal essay differs in purpose because it is designed for entertainment. The author is casual and friendly—often humorous.

Formal essays. The formal essay is written in a strict and organized style. It presents factual information and concentrates on explaining rather than entertaining. A *thesis statement* or topic statement determines the purpose of the essay. The thesis statement is a theory, belief, or opinion about a certain topic and the essay attempts to prove that thesis by presenting evidence and drawing a logical conclusion. The major components of an essay can be outlined simply:

I. Thesis introduction

II. Presentation of facts or evidence in support of the thesis

III. Logical conclusion drawn from facts in support of thesis

Complete these activities.

3.21 Find a formal essay in a magazine or a book or reread the essay reprinted in Language Arts LIFEPAC 803. Answer these questions.

a. What characteristics make this article a formal essay?

_____

_____

b. What is the thesis statement?

_____

_____

Informal Essays. An informal essay is also written to relay information. A personal, friendly style and a more casual treatment of the subject is typical of the informal essay. Humor, irony, and even satire are often elements of the informal essay. The main purpose of the informal essay is to entertain while still making a point or providing a certain slant on a topic.

Complete these activities.

3.22 Find an informal essay in a magazine or a book or reread the informal essays reprinted in Language Arts LIFEPAC 803. Answer these questions.

a. What are the major differences between this essay and the formal essay you read?

_____
_____
_____
_____

b. Which type of essay would be best used to convince others of the deity of Christ?

_____

c. Which type of essay would be best used to persuade the town council to abolish an out-dated requirement that all horses be tied to hitching posts outside church between the hours of 9 a.m. and 2 p.m. every Sunday morning?

_____

AUTOBIOGRAPHIES

An autobiography is a nonfiction form of literature. It is a true account of the author about themself or events directly connected to their life. Specific elements of the autobiography in literature include: setting, time, personal life, turning points, and theme. The setting is the location of the story. A geographic location usually has a great influence on the author's life. The time is also a significant factor. Time includes the historical significance, the social conditions, and the political situations, which can have great impact on the author. The author's personal life is an important element because included in this aspect are the people, friends, and relatives who affect the personality of the writer.

The turning points are the main events in the story of a life. These moments are significant; they may lead the way to success or failure, to happiness or tragedy. The final and the most significant element is the theme. Theme is the effect of the autobiography on the reader. Theme is the total impact of the book and may be inspirational. Theme is what the reader gains from the book—courage, faith, hope, or other valuable qualities of character.

Complete this activity.

3.23 Choose an available autobiography from a library or a reliable online source. Read the autobiography and report on it, in writing, using the following guide:

a. Describe the setting.

_____
_____
_____
_____
_____
_____
_____
_____

b. What is the time setting? What major historical events are occurring at this time?

_____
_____
_____
_____
_____
_____
_____
_____

c. Describe the author's personal life.

_____
_____
_____
_____
_____
_____

d. List some of the major turning points in the author's life.

_____
_____
_____
_____
_____
_____
_____

e. What is the main theme of this autobiography?

_____
_____
_____
_____
_____
_____
_____
_____

f. What is the title of the autobiography and who is it about?

_____
_____

TEACHER CHECK _____   _____
　　　　　　　　　　　　initials　　date

SPELLING

The spelling words from this review are words which contain a silent letter. These words are taken from the Language Arts LIFEPACs 801 through 809.

Unit 10 | **Language Elements in Review**

Spelling Words-3 (Review Words-1)

acquire	pneumonia	exhausted
solemn	isthmus	government
psychology	poignant	lightning
indebtedness	arctic	mathematician
mortgage	arrangement	inhibition
guarantee	eighth	undoubtedly
scissors	exhilarate	maligned
disguise	whether	
writhe	rhyme	

Complete these activities.

3.24 Write each spelling word and underline the silent letter or letters in each.

a. _____ b. _____

c. _____ d. _____

e. _____ f. _____

g. _____ h. _____

i. _____ j. _____

k. _____ l. _____

m _____ n. _____

o. _____ p. _____

q. _____ r. _____

s. _____ t. _____

u. _____ v. _____

w. _____ x. _____

y. _____

3.25 Write a short story on a separate sheet of paper. See how many of your spelling words you can include. Underline the spelling words in your story. Share it with a friend.

HELPER CHECK _____ _____
                   initials   date

Section 3 | **59**

Language Elements in Review | Unit 10

The words in this spelling review have meanings that are related to the study of Language Arts. The words are taken from Language Arts LIFEPACs 801 through 809.

Spelling Words-3 (Review Words-2)

supplement	syllable	parenthesis
library	italics	possessive
asterisk	capitalization	communication
narrative	hyphen	gesture
auxiliary	apostrophe	diction
modifier	prefix	formal
determiners	suffix	homonym
abbreviation	contraction	antonym
quotation marks		

Complete these activities.

3.26 Define or give an example for each word on the spelling list.

a. supplement _____

b. library _____

c. asterisk _____

d. narrative _____

e. auxiliary _____

f. modifier _____

g. determiners _____

h. abbreviation _____

i. quotation marks _____

j. syllable _____

k. italics _____

l. capitalization _____

m. hyphen _____

n. apostrophe _____

o. prefix _____

Unit 10 | **Language Elements in Review**

p. suffix _____

q. contraction _____

r. parenthesis _____

s. possessive _____

t. communication _____

u. gesture _____

v. diction _____

w. formal _____

x. homonym _____

y. antonym _____

3.27 Complete this activity with a helper or a friend. Each person should follow the instructions and exchange papers at the end of the activity. You will each work the puzzle made by the other person. Take at least ten words from the spelling list. Scramble the letters so that the words are out of order. Provide a hint or clue by giving the meaning or an example of the scrambled word. Your clue can be a drawing.

HELPER CHECK _____ _____
                  initials   date

3.28 Review your spelling words in this section by using one or more of these devices. Ask your teacher which one(s) to complete.

a. Have a spelling bee type of competition with some of the members of your class.

b. Review with a friend.

c. Review with your parents.

d. Write each spelling word three times.

ABC **Ask your teacher to give you a practice spelling test of Spelling Words-3.** Restudy the words you missed.

Section 3 | **61**

Language Elements in Review | Unit 10

Before you take this last Self Test, you may want to do one or more of these self checks.

1. _____ Read the objectives. See if you can do them.
2. _____ Restudy the material related to any objectives that you cannot do.
3. _____ Use the **SQ3R** study procedure to review the material:
   a. **S**can the sections.
   b. **Q**uestion yourself.
   c. **R**ead to answer your questions.
   d. **R**ecite the answers to yourself.
   e. **R**eview areas you did not understand.
4. _____ Review all vocabulary, activities, and Self Tests, writing a correct answer for every wrong answer.

Unit 10 | **Language Elements in Review**

SELF TEST 3

Match these items (each answer, 2 points).

3.01	_____ affixes	a.	word for word, exact
3.02	_____ chronological	b.	understanding
3.03	_____ documentation	c.	time order
3.04	_____ lead	d.	a certain bias or point of view
3.05	_____ monotone	e.	proof
3.06	_____ comprehension	f.	exact
3.07	_____ coherence	g.	the first sentence in a news article
3.08	_____ precise	h.	a succession of identical sounds
3.09	_____ slant	i.	order and logic, clarity
3.010	_____ literal	j.	transitions
3.011	_____ morpheme	k.	smallest meaningful language unit
		l.	prefix, suffix, and inflections

Complete these statements (each answer, 3 points).

3.012 The parent language of English was _____ .

3.013 Books that help writers find words are a(n) a. _____ and a(n) b. _____ .

3.014 A word that has the same meaning as another word is a(n) _____ .

3.015 The first step in writing a composition is choosing a(n) _____ .

3.016 Speaking is a form of _____ communication.

3.017 No door is closed to the person who can _____ .

3.018 A lead sentence should include certain information telling a. _____ , b. _____ , c. _____ , d. _____ , e. _____ , and f. _____ .

3.019 In a news article the most important information will be found in the _____ paragraph.

3.020 The style of writing a news article so that it can be edited easily is called _____ writing.

Section 3 | 63

Language Elements in Review | Unit 10

Answer these questions (each answer, 5 points).

3.021 What is the difference between fact and opinion?

_____
_____
_____
_____

3.022 What is the major purpose of a serious essay?

_____
_____
_____

3.023 What are the five specific elements of the autobiography?

a. _____ b. _____

c. _____ d. _____

e. _____

Complete these activities (each part, 3 points).

3.024 List the elements a perfect paragraph should have.

a. _____

b. _____

c. _____

d. _____

3.025 List two ways to arrange information in paragraphs.

a. _____

b. _____

3.026 List three types of sentence errors.

a. _____

b. _____

c. _____

3.027 List two main categories of letters and three examples of each.

a. _____

b. _____

Identify or define these terms (each answer, 4 points).

3.028 pentad _____

3.029 sequence _____

3.030 thesis _____

102/127 SCORE _____ TEACHER _____ _____
                                    initials   date

ABC Take your spelling test of Spelling Words-3.

Before taking the LIFEPAC Test, you may want to do one or more of these self checks.

1. _____ Read the objectives. See if you can do them.
2. _____ Restudy the material related to any objectives that you cannot do.
3. _____ Use the **SQ3R** study procedure to review the material.
4. _____ Review activities, Self Tests, and LIFEPAC vocabulary words.
5. _____ Restudy areas of weakness indicated by the last Self Test.

NOTES